When Sally Kern dared to speak out publicly against the pro-homosexual political movement, she learned an important lesson—that the self-styled apostles of "tolerance" are intolerant of any dissent, and that those who are quickest to cry hate can be the most hateful of all. Their goal is no longer to persuade intellectually or to win politically—it is to silence all opposition. But her opponents learned a lesson too—that this grandmother, high school teacher, and pastor's wife was a woman of courage and faith who would not be intimidated. Her story should serve as both a warning and an inspiration.

—TONY PERKINS
President of Family Research Council

A shocking exposé about retaliation against one woman who stood up for her values.

—PHYLLIS SCHLAFLY
Conservative leader and founder of the Eagle Forum

It is my belief that every American should read *The Stoning of Sally Kern*. As one who struggled with unwanted same-sex attraction but is now free of it, I can bear witness to the truth to be found in this book like few others. Just as my personal freedom from homosexuality came at a cost, our American freedom has come at a cost—and if we are not willing to count that cost, as Sally Kern has, America as we know it is doomed. Full of research on the homosexual agenda—which is a very real agenda—and full of how to respond to this attack on all that is good and decent and right about America, *The Stoning of Sally Kern* is a most valuable tool in preparing the heart and mind for this spiritual and moral battle—a battle we will all be forced to face one day soon whether we like it or not.

—DENNIS JERNIGAN
Songwriter and author

Sally Kern is a modern-day hero—a Joan of Arc for our time! Sally is a woman of courage, compassion, integrity, and intensity, with a mother's motivation to preserve America for the next generation. *The Stoning of Sally Kern* is a must-read to understand the vicious tactics of those who would seize power from the people and how to overcome them. A stirring story of a public schoolteacher and pastor's wife turned Oklahoma State Representative and cultural champion, this book will make your blood boil and then have you on your feet cheering Sally on to victory!

—WILLIAM J. FEDERER
Best-selling author and nationally known speaker

Representative Sally Kern has successfully integrated biblical principles with the philosophy of government set forth by our Founding Fathers to identify the conservative ideology that can restore America to the greatness it has long enjoyed under the blessings of God. This simple but profound philosophy has enabled Sally to withstand unprecedented types of attacks leveled against her by homosexual activists. *The Stoning of Sally Kern* will not only open your eyes to a real threat facing America, but it will also encourage and motivate traditional, God-fearing Americans to stand boldly against attacks on our faith and the faith of our fathers.

—DAVID BARTON
Founder of WallBuilders

Throughout the Bible, God has called the most humble of people to step into the spotlight and carry His banner forward. Moses was an eighty-year-old flock herder, David was a shepherd boy, and Peter was a fisherman. All were content with their lives and minding their own business when God called them into controversy for righteousness' sake. Sally Kern is just such a modern-day example—a pastor's wife and schoolteacher called into public service and thrust into the spotlight of the spiritual battle for morality in America. You will love this compelling testimony from a faithful servant of the Lord Jesus Christ.

—PASTOR PAUL BLAIR
Executive director of Reclaiming America for Christ
and founder of Reclaiming Oklahoma for Christ

I was before her time, but Sally Kern is here *for such a time as this*. I am grateful for her life and her friendship. Reading *The Stoning of Sally Kern* was at times like déjà vu, reminding me of my stand in Dade County in 1977. I can highly recommend this book to anyone who loves God, their family, and their country. It is a must-read for any believing woman or man who wants to make a difference in these perilous times. Those soldiers who have counted the cost of character assassination or endured other losses yet are willing to take a stand in truth and love for the glory of God, our children, and future generations will especially enjoy this inspiring book.

—ANITA BRYANT
Singer and activist

The Stoning of Sally Kern is a book that can't be put aside until the last page. Throughout history there have been those few people who inspired the rest of us to look to our better selves. Such people are God's special folks whom He uses to show that we *can* stand firm on His Word for those things that are right—even in the face of sure opposition and criticism. This story about a modern-day Joan of Arc named Sally Kern is an inspiring example to each of us that such courage is still alive in America.

The Stoning of Sally Kern is a page-turner. I recommend sending a copy to your relatives, pastor, and even people you don't know. America needs more Sally Kerns. Christians need to know that the spirit of the boy David in his battle with the giants of his time is not dead today. Just as God used him, He also used Sally Kern. And He will use each one of us if we follow His plan for our lives. Sally Kern's book will come alive in your own life as you read her story.

—DICK BOTT SR.
Founder of Bott Radio Network

THE
STONING
OF
SALLY KERN

Ruth,
Stand strong for
God's Word & America

For God & Country

Sally Kern

2011

THE STONING OF SALLY KERN

SALLY KERN

OKLAHOMA STATE REPRESENTATIVE, HOUSE DISTRICT 84

Most CHARISMA HOUSE BOOK GROUP products are available at special quantity discounts for bulk purchase for sales promotions, premiums, fund-raising, and educational needs. For details, write Charisma House Book Group, 600 Rinehart Road, Lake Mary, Florida 32746, or telephone (407) 333-0600.

THE STONING OF SALLY KERN by Sally Kern
Published by FrontLine
Charisma Media/Charisma House Book Group
600 Rinehart Road
Lake Mary, Florida 32746
www.charismahouse.com

Unless otherwise noted, all Scripture quotations are from the Holman Christian Standard Bible. Copyright © 1999, 2000, 2002, 2003 by Holman Bible Publishers, Nashville, Tennessee. All rights reserved.

Scripture quotations marked KJV are from the King James Version of the Bible.

Scripture quotations marked NIV are from the Holy Bible, New International Version. Copyright © 1973, 1978, 1984, International Bible Society. Used by permission.

Cover design by Studio Gearbox
Design Director: Bill Johnson

Visit the author's website at www.repsallykern.com.

EDITOR'S NOTE: Historical quotes have been conformed to original documents, using archaic spelling and capitalization.

Library of Congress Cataloging-in-Publication Data
Kern, Sally.
   The stoning of Sally Kern / Sally Kern. -- 1st ed.
      p. cm.
   Includes bibliographical references (p.   ) and index.
   ISBN 978-1-61638-361-9 (hardback) -- ISBN 978-1-61638-438-8 (e-book)
1. Conservatism--Religious aspects--Christianity. 2.
Conservatism--United States--History--21st century. 3. Christianity and
politics--United States. 4. United States--Church history--21st
century. 5. United States--Politics and government--21st century. 6.
Homosexuality--Religious aspects--Christianity. 7. Kern, Sally. I.
Title.
   BR115.C66K47 2011
   261.710973--dc22
                                        2011010008

First Edition

11 12 13 14 15 — 9 8 7 6 5 4 3 2 1
Printed in the United States of America

Dedication

THERE ARE A NUMBER OF PEOPLE I WISH TO DEDICATE THIS book to because if not for them it never would have been written. I am eternally grateful to each for the part they played in this endeavor.

First and foremost is my wonderful husband, Dr. Steve Kern. This book was his brainchild. He took the initiative to seek out people who might be interested in such a work. He also was the slave driver who unrelentingly stood over me for those months it took to write it. At times he was a real nuisance, but I thank God for him because he understood that time was of the essence.

Next is my family. Jesse, our oldest son, whose reputation and character have been tested through these recent events, still insisted I write this book. He knows that his mom and dad love him dearly and would never disown him, no matter what. Nathan, our other son, and his wife, Amie, who had to put up with listening to all the insults, also answered questions from their friends about what kind of mom and mother-in-law they have. They encouraged me countless times to hang in there.

Then there is T. J. King, my legislative assistant at the capitol who is, without a doubt, now qualified to be a bodyguard. At the office she was my shield in the midst of the storm. I appreciate her more than she'll ever know.

All of you from all parts of the globe who prayed for me are a part of this book, especially those of you from our church, Olivet Baptist

Church. Your prayers provided encouragement, a hedge of protection, and an infusion of God's strength and peace without which I could not have faced each new day.

My fellow representatives who stood with me through this—you know who you are. It meant a lot to me to know you were there. I owe a special thanks to Rep. Ann Coody, who also took the time to edit the manuscript and make it better.

Lastly, and you may think this really odd, I want to dedicate this book to the homosexual community who took offense at my words. Had you not been offended, this book would not have been written. God has used this experience to teach me many things about Him, myself, and about you and the struggles you face. I have grown and matured in ways I never thought possible. Although I am accused of being filled with hate toward you, God has actually given me a love and compassion for you that I would not have had otherwise.

Ultimately, I dedicate this book to my Lord and Savior, Jesus Christ. My prayer is that He will be lifted up through it and that people will be drawn to Him because of it.

Contents

Introduction

I NERVOUSLY STEERED MY CAR AROUND THE FINAL CORNER OF MY drive home from the Oklahoma State Capitol and took one more glance into the rearview mirror to see if anyone was following me. Looking down the street toward my house, I quickly scanned for unfamiliar cars or for vans with microwave antennae on their roofs from the local television network affiliates. In both cases I was relieved to see nothing.

As the garage door closed behind me, I shut my eyes and breathed a deep, weary sigh of relief. Here, for a quiet moment or two, there were no harassing phone calls or requests for media interviews. For a minute there in my quiet sanctuary I was just little old Sally Kern again—a pastor's wife, an inner-city high school teacher, and a doting grandmother.

Another deep breath, a whispered prayer for strength, and I walked inside and sat down at the computer. Opening my e-mail application, I found just what the previous forty-eight hours had trained me to expect. The in-box counter for my account as a legislator in the Oklahoma House of Representatives indicated an avalanche of e-mail—the figure of unread messages had hit a thousand and was climbing. Two thousand unread messages. Three thousand. They just kept coming.

I had also come to know and dread what those messages would contain. They were being sent from all over the United States, the world actually, and the overwhelming majority of them would accuse me of being a horrible, demented person—and they would do so using some of the filthiest language imaginable. Many of them would say I deserved to die. It was surreal and, frankly, terrifying.

There's that old saying, "Sticks and stones may break my bones, but words will never hurt me." Yet as I sat there reading some of those e-mails, each one hit me like a sharp stone, breaking my heart and filling my eyes with tears. I had never experienced such hate or seen such vulgarity in my life. The hurt seemed to cut right into my soul. It was not just that I was being hurt, but that the truth of God's Word was being stoned and desecrated. This fact pierced all the way through into my spirit and produced an element of fear in me. I was fearful of the reality of living in a world where God's Word is no longer honored or held in reverence.

You may be wondering, "What could you possibly have done to trigger such rage?" The answer makes for an interesting story, and I plan to tell it.

I'm an ordinary person of average abilities with typical dreams and hopes. But since March 7, 2008, my life has been anything but ordinary, average, or typical. Never in my wildest dreams did I even once imagine what could happen to me because of a few hurried remarks I made in a speech to a handful of people.

Read on, and I'll tell you a remarkable, true story of how I was verbally stoned when I stumbled into the crosshairs of a global network of angry bloggers, well-financed political conspiracies, and even a famous talk show host. Yes, on the pages that follow I will tell you the bizarre story of my lightning-fast rise (or descent) from a cookie-baking grandma to a pop culture pariah.

But this story is not just about me. It's about anyone who still believes in the truth of God's Word. There is a war going on for the soul of this nation, and the liberal attack on conservative Christian values is relentless.

As you read this book, I hope you will be inspired and challenged by what I've gone through and that you, probably just an ordinary person like me, will take your stand. If you do, and if you become engaged in this battle, your life will be changed too. If enough of us take a stand, it will change the very future of our nation.

It is my prayer that this book will be an alarm to alert us of impending danger for America. We can't just go about our everyday activities as if there were no stealthy schemes of attack unfolding against America's Christian foundations. The kind of future our children will inherit depends upon it.

Chapter One

"GOOD LORD, WHAT HAVE I DONE?"

AN ICY KNOT FORMED IN MY STOMACH AS I SNAPPED my mobile phone closed and laid it on the car seat beside me. It was March 7, 2008, and as long as I live I'll remember the petrifying feeling of fear and confusion that penetrated my whole body.

It was a Friday, my day off since the Oklahoma state legislature doesn't meet on Fridays and my weekends tend to be full of the responsibilities that come with being a pastor's wife. So I was out running errands.

Since 2004, I have served as a state representative for House District 84 covering parts of northwest Oklahoma City. It was a little after 1:00 p.m. on this day when TJ, my legislative assistant at the Oklahoma State Capitol, called me with a clear note of alarm, bordering on panic, in her voice. "Sally, we're getting thousands, and I mean *thousands* of e-mails. And they're not just e-mails but–but hate e-mails."

I couldn't believe what I was hearing. There had to be some sort of mistake. "From whom?" I asked her.

"From angry homosexuals mostly," she said. She went on to explain that apparently someone had secretly recorded one of my talks to a group of grassroots Republican activists and that segments of it had been edited together and put on YouTube for all the world to hear. My mind raced as I tried to recall the various speaking engagements I'd had recently and what I'd said in each of them.

My next thought following the initial wave of fear was, "Good Lord, what have I done?"

INFAMOUS

In the span of a few short days in March 2008, I became more than famous. I found myself instantly *infamous*.

From sea to shining sea, I was suddenly being reviled, denounced, and despised. One week I was Little Mrs. Nobody out in flyover country. The next week I was being demonized in a YouTube video that, as of this writing, has been viewed more than 1.2 million times. At broadband speed, the World Wide Web lit up with contempt for "that hateful Sally Kern." Google my name, and you'll be presented with links to tens of thousands of blog posts and articles with headlines such as "Sally Kern: Bashing Gays for Jesus" and "Terrorists Among Us: Rep. Sally Kern."

Gossip blogger Perez Hilton took a break from virtually stalking Hollywood celebrities in order to opine that the people of Oklahoma should be ashamed of me. Ellen DeGeneres devoted a segment of her television program to mocking me and trying to call me on the phone. These high-profile attacks triggered a tsunami of e-mail filled with the vilest and most defiling obscenities imaginable.

Of course, all of this attention was unplanned, unanticipated, and unprepared for. It was also extraordinarily hurtful, not just to me but to the people I love most in this world. It's painful to be accused of hate when you know there is no hate in your heart. It's discouraging to have your words twisted and exploited in the ears of the entire nation. And it is maddening to have a grotesque caricature of yourself paraded around as genuine by thousands of people who don't know the first thing about you.

As my story unfolds, you will see that my stand is not against individuals but against the forces that would seek to undermine the truth of God's Word. This nation was founded on biblical principles, and that is what has made America strong. Our Founding Fathers recognized that there are social, economic, and cultural benefits of Christian values that bring blessings to the nation that embraces them. This was the foundation of the now infamous speech that thrust me into the limelight, but of course, that part wasn't plastered all over YouTube.

Amid the hailstorm of name-calling and derision that came my way, one of the least obscene and most commonly used labels was that of "homophobe." In fact, I was named the runner-up for "Homophobe of the Year" by a certain national homosexual organization's website.

It has become common in recent years to slap the label of "homophobe" on anyone who objects to open homosexuality on moral or religious grounds or to the homosexual activists' political agenda on ideological grounds. It's a clever tactic—repeatedly assigning the label of a neurosis or mental illness to those who disagree with you. You don't have to engage "crazy people" in debate on the merits of the issues. You just marginalize them and dismiss them.

Of course, a phobia is, by definition, an irrational fear. But the concerns I have about the radical homosexual lobby's political agenda and the effect it will have on future generations are hardly irrational. They are grounded in facts and are quite rational.

Based on the hysterical reactions I've experienced to a few poorly worded comments I made, however, it's fair to wonder if some people don't indeed have an irrational fear of morality-based arguments. Perhaps some people are "holyphobes." In a different sense, you might call me a holyphobe, in that I have reverential fear of God. I care more about what God thinks of my life and actions than how any living person on this earth views them.

In any event, I've certainly grown weary of being called a homophobe. The truth is, I don't hate or fear homosexuals, or anyone else for that matter. Disagreeing with someone does not mean you hate him. I was not brought up to hate people. My parents taught each of their children that everyone is worthy of love and respect just because they are created by God and are of great value to Him. My husband and I sought to rear our children with the same understanding. If I'm not willing to love others regardless of who they are or what they might do, then how can I expect God to love me?

What concerns me is the damage that will be done to America's moral fiber and to religious freedom if we succumb to attacks on our conservative Christian foundations. In the chapters that follow I will reveal how a highly organized, well-funded network of radical activists is working to undermine our God-given liberties in the name of equality and freedom. Speaking out about these facts is what put me in the crosshairs of the liberal blogosphere and even caused some to label me an extreme danger to Western civilization.

In reality, I'm about as ordinary as you can get. I have no fantastic talents, I look like a typical sixty-something grandmother, and though I was smart enough to get a college degree and teach government to a couple generations of high school kids, I've never been offered membership in the Mensa IQ society or been accused of being an intellectual. Just ordinary. Average. Typical. That's me.

This whole experience has taken me completely by surprise. As a result, the last few years have had a surreal quality to them. I'm just now beginning to realize that this is probably the way it's going to be for the rest of my life, even when I'm no longer a state representative. I think I can relate just a little bit to what Sarah Palin experienced.

A New Kind of War

There was a day that took the United States by surprise. It was December 7, 1941, when Japan bombed Pearl Harbor. Prior to that fateful day Americans knew a war was taking place, but most didn't think it involved them. As long as the fighting was going on someplace overseas far away, they didn't really care about it, and so they were just living their lives and going about their everyday activities. But that changed in a heartbeat when, unexpectedly, the planes roared down, and our mothers and fathers, sons and daughters, brothers and sisters were under attack without any warning and little chance to fight back.

There is a war going on today, and, just like on December 7, 1941, most Americans are going to be totally surprised at the devastation and change that is going to take place in our nation. The difference between this current attack and the one on Pearl Harbor is that the enemy is living and fighting right here among us, but we don't recognize them. The hard reality is that the enemy could be connected to your mother or father, sons or daughters, brothers or sisters, or coworkers. That's what makes this war so hard to fight. It can feel as if we're fighting those we love.

The real enemy, however, is not these loved ones but a worldview that is being strategically implemented in our homes, schools, churches, and governments. This is a war for the soul of our nation, and it is a whole new experience for Americans.

This is why the experience I'm going through is not just about me. It's about something much bigger and more important than me or even you. This is about our future and what we will leave to generations that follow. The statements I made in my speech and the actions

I've taken since then have forever altered my life. My future has been changed. It's been changed for the better, although that's not what my opponents intended. They did not take into account the divine promise of Romans 8:28—that God works all things together for the good of those who love Him.

Sometimes we do things that, in the moment, seem inconsequential to us, but God takes them and turns them into defining moments in our lives. Little did I know that the secretly recorded remarks I had made represented such a moment.

Before I share with you the comments that generated such a firestorm of abuse, allow me to give you some of the background behind them. Back in October 2007 I attended a ProFamily Legislators Conference. There I learned of a group of very wealthy homosexual activists who had stealthily targeted seventy conservative political officials across the nation to defeat them in state and local elections. Their goal was, and is, to completely change the American political landscape from the bottom up over the next ten years in order to create a friendlier legislative environment for their agenda.

There were six other Oklahoma legislators who attended that conference and received the same information I heard. But I was the only one who came back home with the motivation to do more research on the subject. "Why me, Lord?" I wondered. That's a question I've asked myself many times since March 7, 2008.

That day in the car, I couldn't wait to get off the phone with TJ and call Steve, my husband. As my best friend and biggest supporter when I was running for the House of Representatives, I desperately needed his wisdom and counsel. Still feeling very much afraid, I shared with him the conversation TJ and I had just had. I recall that Steve asked me, "Do you know which meeting they recorded?" You see, I had given this same basic speech on four different occasions. Evidently it wasn't just grassroots Republican activists who found it interesting.

As Steve and I prayed together over the phone, the peace of God that passes all understanding began to displace the paralyzing fear I was experiencing. As a minister's wife I had talked hundreds of times about the peace of God. But in that moment I learned the sweet reality of the indescribable contrast between heavenly peace and worldly fear.

As we continued talking, TJ called again. "Sally," she said as I dropped Steve's call and took hers, "you just got a call from…" Then she said the name of a highly aggressive local homosexual activist. "He said to tell you that you were going to be more famous than you ever dreamed you'd be because he was going to send that YouTube clip to all three thousand people on his e-mail list."

"Famous," I thought to myself. "This is not exactly the way I had ever imagined I'd be famous." As I mentioned in the introduction, I'd never coveted or pursued fame. Now it looked as though I was going to be famous for "ticking off" the world's homosexual population, and all I did was share with a small group of people what some liberal homosexual millionaires were doing.

TJ then told me that reporters were beginning to call the office wanting to know if it was indeed my voice on the YouTube video. Of course, I didn't know whether it was my voice or not. And as a sixty-one-year-old grandmother who was pretty close to being computer illiterate, I didn't even know how to get on to YouTube to check. So there on my cell phone, sitting in the parking lot at Walmart, I waited anxiously while TJ got online and pulled up the YouTube clip. As she put the phone next to the computer's speakers, I listened intently, straining to hear every word. I also was quietly hoping and praying that there had been some mistake and the voice wouldn't be mine.

No such luck.

After confirming that the voice on the other end of the phone was mine, I had TJ transfer me to our legal staff at the capitol. I figured that it might be a good idea to see if they had any advice for me.

While I waited to be connected, I lifted my voice up to the Lord in prayer. "Father, I've said over and over that Your grace is sufficient. If there was ever a time I needed Your grace, it's now."

As I related to the staff lawyer the events of the last few moments, I was told that, in her opinion, there was nothing that could be done. No laws appeared to have been broken by anyone. I was inwardly hoping that she would have some simple and magical solution that would make all this go away as quickly as it had appeared.

Again, no such luck.

At this point you might be thinking that this was not my lucky day. Thankfully I don't believe luck is what guides my life. The next phone call I made was going to confirm that belief.

Feeling much calmer now but still trying to wrap my mind around all that was happening, I really felt impressed to make one more call. I don't know why, but I did, and it proved to be the call that gave me a sense of purpose for what was occurring.

Not really grasping that I was now squarely embroiled in a major controversy, this next call was to an individual who *is* controversial in Oklahoma politics. If you're an elected official in Oklahoma, you either hate or love Charlie Meadows. There's no in-between. As the longtime chairman of the Oklahoma Conservative Political Action Committee (OCPAC), Charlie gives no slack to any elected official.

I dialed Charlie's number, and he answered right away. I told him about the YouTube video and all the hate e-mail I was getting. Charlie had heard my speech on the homosexual agenda three times. The first sentence out of his mouth was, "Praise the Lord, He's given you a platform to poke your finger in their eye—figuratively speaking, of course." This blunt statement startled me and pierced my heart. And I suddenly recognized that the Lord had set the stage for a confrontation between the truth of His Word and the lies of this present age.

Of course, this is not a new battle. Ephesians 6:10–18 clearly asserts that this war has been going on for all time. What was new was that God had just called me up as one of His frontline soldiers in the battle for truth. Seems the Lord was taking me at my word. You see, when I first campaigned for office, I had my spiel down pat when I knocked on thousands of voters' doors. It went like this: "I'm running as a decidedly Christian candidate because I believe we're in a cultural war for the very existence of our Judeo-Christian values." I made that statement in 2003 because I believed it. Now I was being asked to live it.

It is a biblical principle that the spoken word has power. Sometimes God takes what we say and creates opportunities to exhibit His power. Before the day was out, I'd had three TV stations call asking for interviews. I hate doing TV interviews. I don't like the way my voice sounds. My hair never looks right. And the cameraman always gets right up in my face. They do that when they're trying to make a person look bad. I felt certain that the media would attempt to make me look as bad as possible. I was not disappointed.

There was a common thread in all the media interviews I did in those first hours and days. Invariably I would get questions along the lines of, "Is that *really* what you meant to say?" Or, "Would you like to clarify your statements?"

As I've already stated, the comments that were secretly recorded were rushed, and I could have done a better job of making a few of my points, and I said so. But reporters never seemed satisfied with that explanation. It quickly became clear to me that what these media folks were looking for was a retraction. The fact was, I was being invited, encouraged, prodded, and subtly coached to *recant*! And that I could not in good conscience do.

I kept thinking about something I read that nineteenth-century abolitionist preacher James Freeman Clarke once said: "The politician thinks of the next election; the statesman, of the next century."[1] I wasn't really interested in preserving my position; I was passionately committed to preserving my country. So I hardheadedly refused to say that I had "misspoken" or to use any of the other weasel words we're accustomed to hearing politicians hide behind.

The more I stuck to my guns, however, the more hostile and slanted the media coverage became.

TAKING A STAND

When I got home and put my groceries away, I went straight to the computer to check my Oklahoma House of Representatives e-mail account. I was not prepared for what I saw. It was one thing to hear TJ say I was getting thousands of e-mails. It was another thing to actually see them pouring into my in-box. But the quantity was not the problem. It was the content. I was being accused of "hate speech" for merely citing what was already written in various articles in mainstream publications, such as the *Atlantic Monthly* and *Time* magazine online, and for what the Centers for Disease Control and Prevention had on its website for anyone to see with a few clicks of a mouse.

These facts were "inconvenient truths," to borrow a phrase, that some groups don't want advertised. Of course, the writers of the e-mails were especially enraged that I had compared homosexuality to terrorism and to a cancer, two things that destroy. That's what really set them off.

Without a doubt, I had hit a nerve. I found it sort of ironic that those who were consistently most vocal in calling for hate crimes laws and in preaching tolerance were the very people sending me thousands of e-mails filled with some of the most obscene words and vicious sentiments I'd ever seen. There was absolutely no tolerance for *my* choices or beliefs. As a high school teacher, I thought I knew all of the profane and vile words out there. But while sitting at my computer for thirty minutes, reading some of those e-mails, I saw more vulgar words in that time than I'd seen in all my life.

As I continued to wade through the avalanche of profane contempt, my stomach had a large and growing knot in the middle of it. I can't adequately describe the way I felt—a queasy mixture of fear, confusion, and defilement. I just knew I needed the Lord to calm my spirit, give me His strength, and fill me with love for these people.

I had no clue about what the future would hold as a result of becoming a visible target of the activist homosexual community. One thing I did know: God honors His Word. I knew that I could not back down from the truth of His Word. No matter what it may cost me, I would rather be biblically correct than politically correct. I also knew that God loves the homosexual just as He loves me. God loves all people. But He doesn't love sinful actions. I knew that I had to keep this uppermost in my mind if God was to be glorified through all this.

As I quickly discovered, not only was hate e-mail being sent to my state legislative e-mail account, but also the activist networks somehow had obtained my home e-mail address too. It immediately became almost impossible to sift through all the garbage and find the legitimate e-mail from friends and family. Those who had been offended by my remarks also began calling our home phone at all hours of the day and night, leaving the filthiest messages I'd ever heard. I was surely thankful we didn't have little children at home to hear that vile language.

The next day, as the gravity of this situation began to dawn on us, Steve and I sat down together and counted the cost. It was a process we understood well. Many years ago after we were first married, we were in a ministry where we gave up all we possessed (which wasn't much at the time) and worked with street kids. This was a step into what some call "full-faith" ministry because we were totally dependent upon God to meet our needs. The young people we were ministering among were the Jesus people of the 1970s. But following that path meant giving up pretty much everything. Thus we had engaged in a serious count-the-cost exercise before that leap of faith.

Those years of street ministry turned out to be a wonderful experience, and God has since allowed us to possess a home, autos, and all the stuff that we think we must have today. In the midst of this new crisis, Steve asked me if I was willing to lose it all again. I told him I was. Then I told him that if standing for righteousness cost me my seat as a state representative, I couldn't think of a better reason to lose it. The next question was a much more sobering one, but answering it gave us an overwhelming sense of peace and boldness. The question was, "And what if it costs us our lives?"

The levels of irrational hate and rage that were being poured upon us certainly made it conceivable that we might be the targets of violence. Indeed we had already seen some thinly veiled threats. Assured of an eternal home in heaven and mindful of those throughout church history who laid down their lives for the faith, we both agreed to stand—whatever the cost.

We just sat there in silence for a while. Then Steve prayed, asking God to give us His strength and love to face this in a way that would please Him.

I can't really explain how liberating it was to count the cost that Saturday night. We were both humbled that, for whatever reason, God had allowed this situation to take place in our lives.

Although events were happening in rapid-fire succession that first week, the days went by with painful slowness. I did so many TV interviews that I quickly lost count as the days became a blur of TV lights and microphones. I just know I finally quit giving them because they never let me explain my side of the story or seemed to give me a fair shake. Sad to say, they didn't really want the truth. They either just wanted a story—something that would get them viewers—or they were philosophically sympathetic to the homosexual rights cause.

I do vividly recall the reporter who blindsided me with her last question. It went something like this, "I hear you have a son who's gay. Is that true?" I was stunned and, frankly, angered by the question. I flatly told her that what she had heard was not true. I quickly added that if it were true, I would love him all the more because he would need more loving. If I remember correctly, I also told her that she was doing a poor job of journalism because it sounded more like she was working for the *National Inquirer* rather than a legitimate news station. Just as a mother bear will roar to protect her cubs, my motherly instinct had been called up. Pick on me all you want, but leave my family out of this.

Apparently, the moment I got in the crosshairs of the homosexual rights activists, enterprising researchers started digging through my life for dirt. It must have been a frustrating and disappointing search. As I've already mentioned, I've been a pastor's wife in an inner-city church and a public schoolteacher. My husband and I have spent a major part of our lives in inner-city ministry—clothing and feeding the poor, helping the homeless, ministering to the drug addicts, and reaching out with help and hope to AIDS sufferers.

There simply was not "dirt" in my life for the press to play with. Yet when they learned that one of my sons is thirty-something and single, they jumped to the most convenient and appealing (for their purposes) conclusion. "Aha!" they seem to have told themselves. "We knew this Sally Kern was a hypocrite!" (In the worldview they have constructed for themselves, all outspoken Christians are.) Soon, key blogs popular with the homosexual activist community were posting reports, usually citing each other as confirmation, that "Sally Kern has a gay son" and that "she has disowned him."

Of course, neither part of that smear is true. How shamefully vicious to drag my children into a campaign to defame and/or silence me. How ironic that many of the individuals repeating these slurs frequently offer high-minded rhetoric about respecting the privacy rights of individuals.

Nevertheless, this has become a familiar mode of operation by those on the far-left fringes of the culture wars. Digging for dirt and making stuff up if it can't be found is only one familiar tactic of this movement. High-profile mockery is another.

THE COST OF OBEDIENCE

One morning during that first week Ellen DeGeneres called my office from the set of her television program. However, as I was getting calls from all over the nation telling me what a horrible person I was, my voice-mail box was full, and she was not able to get through. You may have seen the episode of her show as she made the call. She's shown it more than once. To begin the segment, she played the YouTube recording while showing my picture. Injecting her signature humor at various points, she had her entire audience laughing at me. Making anyone who disagrees with the homosexual lifestyle look like a fool is a major tactic of homosexual activists. Ellen was employing that tactic superbly.

Next I got a call from the *Dr. Phil Show*. I seriously considered returning his call because he seems to give people a fair shake on his program. Instead, I had one of the media staff make the call to see just what he had in mind. We were told that there would probably be a panel of people from both sides of the issue to discuss the topic. I've seen a few of those types of shows, and they seem to end up in shouting matches—shedding much more heat than light on the subject under discussion. I have no problem with an honest discourse on the topic, but I was afraid that this situation might be more for show than a rational dialogue. So I declined the opportunity to appear on the *Dr. Phil Show*.

Besides, as I've said, this is not about me. Having my picture flashed all over international TV on CNN, the *Ellen DeGeneres Show*, and hundreds of homosexual blogs is more than enough bad publicity to last a lifetime. What I'm interested in is being obedient to God and His Word. I had no idea what being obedient would cost me. Scripture says that Jesus humbled Himself by becoming obedient to the point of death. To be honest, I sincerely hoped that my obedience wouldn't cost me that. Yet that's what happens to soldiers in war. Jesus laid down His life for me, and I had to be willing to lay down mine if He allowed that. Steve and I had faced this question on that Saturday night and had God's peace. We would take one day at a time, trusting God to protect us with each step.

Chapter Two

THE SPEECH THAT
STARTED IT ALL

S O JUST WHAT WAS ALL THE FUSS ABOUT? JUST WHAT DID I SAY
in the speech that so enraged the homosexual community?
Before we go further on this journey, you should have an answer to
those questions, so I'm printing my now infamous speech for you to
read yourself.

THREE MINUTES THAT CHANGED MY LIFE

First, it is important that I give you a little background and context.
As I've said, I'm just an ordinary person with limited oratory skills,
and when you read the speech, you'll have no doubt that I am telling
the truth about that. Even by my modest standards, I personally think
it is one of the worst speeches I've ever given.

This was one of four occasions on which I had been invited to
share some of the disturbing revelations about a homosexual political strategy that I had learned about at that pro-family conference.
On this and the other three occasions I spoke from outlined notes
rather than from a written, prepared text. On the other occasions, I

had spoken for about forty-five minutes. On the day of this speech, I learned shortly before the event that I would have less than half that time.

At that point I made a critical mistake, though my intentions were good. Given the reduced time allotment, I should have cut my outline down by half. But I had so much important information to deliver, I couldn't bear to think of leaving anything out. So I decided, foolishly, to just try to hurry through my material. Rushing through my notes resulted in my misspeaking twice and my using imprecise language in several other spots. (I have noted these verbal stumbles in the text of the speech below.) Naturally, my critics have really played upon these mistakes in order to make me look ridiculous.

So here it is—the full transcript of my now infamous January 10, 2008, speech:

> Uh…well first, I have gotten some bills passed into law, and secondly I was talking with Bill Graves (my predecessor) once, and he said, "I think you're doing a good job and you kind of took up my program." And I said, "Well, Bill, thank you, but I'd like to think that it's somebody bigger than your program that I'm doing" [i.e., God's]. But anyway, I am thankful to be here today and I am going to share a number of things, so I hope your ears are turned on fast because I want to get through this quickly and I do have…[handouts]. The teacher in me didn't pass these out in advance because I know you'd look at them and read them and not listen to me, and I want you to listen too, but I have some information you want to be sure to get, three handouts over there.
>
> I like to call myself a social conservative, OK, and for me a social conservative is more than just being pro-life and wanting smaller government and spending less. It's

a whole lot more than that. To me, being a government teacher and a history teacher for about twenty years and loving the beginnings of our nation, I believe being a social conservative, you have to embrace the principles upon which this nation was founded if you're going to be a true social conservative.

Now I'd like to start by asking you a question, and I'm not going to give you time to answer because I'll probably, I'll try to finish before one, so if you have any questions you'll have time to ask me. I have no trouble talking. Being a schoolteacher and a minister's wife, talking just comes with the territory.

But if I were to ask you, "What is the one thing that has made America great, that makes us unique, what would it be?" And then if I were to ask you, "What is the one thing that is actually destroying this nation?" What would be your answer? Now I'm not going to let you give me an answer. Charlie's already got his hand up. But I'm not going to let you give me an answer 'cause I'm just going to tell you what I think the one thing is. Actually what made us great and what is destroying is just like a coin; it's a flip side. What made us great is that we were a nation founded on Christian principles. OK, that's just the bottom line. If you go to the primary sources and read our Founding Fathers, what they had to say, they gave preferential treatment to Christianity.

They believed, I'm going to share with you in just a minute, five practical benefits of Christianity. So what's destroying this nation? The fact that we're leaving the roots upon which we were founded. We are crumbling from within because of the bankruptcy that we have in the moral fiber of this nation and leaving the principles of our Founding Fathers. Now I'm going to give away this little booklet, and I don't know how we're going to do it, but you know I'll let Tom figure that out. It's by David Barton, *The Practical Benefits of Christianity*. It's awesome.

I'm briefly going to go through the five practical benefits. You see the thing about religion, religion isn't just spiritual; it's practical. What we have in our society today is a dichotomy. If you're a religious person, that's personal beliefs and that's kinda like in, you know, private, that's in the upper story. But if you're in government, if you're in school, business, that's where facts are, and you don't mix the two. Well, you guys, truth is truth. It doesn't matter what realm of society you are in, truth is truth. There's total truth. If you've never read the book by Nancy Pearcey called *Total Truth*, you need to read that book. Awesome book. *Total Truth*, Nancy Pearcey.

But there are practical benefits to Christianity. Our Founding Fathers knew that, and that's why they chose Christianity, the principles of Christianity, and most of our Founding Fathers were believers in Jesus Christ. That's documented; it's not just hearsay. It's documented.

What are the five practical benefits? First is a civilized society. And civilized, according to the Webster's dictionary, 1828 dictionary, "civilized" means decent, respectful, moral behavior. That's what civilized means. And we can stop and look at our society today, and we don't have a very civilized society because we can see all kinds of depravity all the time. Our Founding Fathers believed that our government was a self-government, and you can only have self-government if you have individual governance in your own life. And the less people are controlled by inner restraints, the more government you have to have to control them. That's just...we see that happening all the time. So they believed that we needed a civilized society. They also believed that Christian principles were the very reason for the way that our society was going to exist is because, and it goes back again to, you have to have self-governance.

One of our first Speakers of the House, and I never can remember his name, but he said men will be governed either by internal restraints or external restraints, either by the bayonet or by the Bible. So we need to have the principles of Christianity for our society to exist.

Another practical benefit of Christianity is just good citizenship. Good citizens, OK. You know it doesn't matter if we live next door to an atheist, an infidel, or whatever, if they believe in a basic principle of right and wrong, which used to always be the Ten Commandments, if they're not going to come over and kill me or steal my stuff, or go after my husband and things like that, I can live next to them. No problem. People used to know what was right and what was considered wrong. Today, it's left up to anybody's, you know, discretion, and that won't work.

Another practical benefit of Christianity was the elevation of knowledge, of learning, of science, OK, of the arts. They believed, matter of fact, Thomas Paine, who wrote *Age of Reason*, where he tried to say you don't need religion, you should keep it out of the public sector. Ben Franklin wrote him a letter—and Ben Franklin, arguably, is one of our lesser considered religious leaders—but he said to Thomas Paine, "Don't write that book; don't publish that book." He said, "It will do you harm; it will do our nation harm." You know, he believed that we needed to have a society that was based upon Christian principles because elevation of science, elevation of knowledge is very important if you're going to have an informed public. And I believe it was Thomas Paine [who] also said, you know, you can look at a picture, and it makes you think of the artist; you can look at some kind of invention, and you think of the inventor. Why is it that we look at the creation, and we don't think about the Creator? You know, we don't do that. And if we really had Christian principles, our educational system would not be in the mess it is in today. I could give you lots of quotes about, oh, Benjamin Rush and Noah Webster and Fisher Ames, who actually penned the First Amendment, the things they had to say about the main book in school should be the Bible. There's a lot of stuff about that that's really important, and we certainly got away from it.

Another practical benefit, the last one, of Christianity, is a cohesive value system. A cohesive value system, we don't have that today. And you know we think, "We hear this all the time; we are such a large society today; we have such diversity in all these different religions and ethnic backgrounds and everything; you can't have a cohesive value system." Well, we didn't just have that right now. You can go back, read some of the writings of John Adams, and he talks about the diverse society that they had back at the beginning of this nation. So Christian principles are very important in order to have a cohesive value system. So regardless of what your faith is, you can live together. We have gotten away from these principles, and it is affecting our lives today.

One of the main ways, and this is something I'm going to talk about a lot today, that is affecting our lives, is in the gay agenda. Now I'm not a gay basher, OK. When I taught school, three doors down from me was one of the most obnoxious gay people that you can mention. If I named him, you probably have seen him. He writes in the paper all the time and everything. But you know, he has the right to practice that lifestyle if he chooses, but he does not have the right to indoctrinate his classes. You know, that's not what education is about. But what we see happening today is the homosexual agenda is destroying this nation. OK, it's just a fact. If you've never read, here's another book, *The Criminalization of Christianity* by Janet Folger. Every Christian ought to read that book, *The Criminalization of Christianity*. It is an awesome book, and if that doesn't scare you and motivate you, something's wrong.

And here's the problem: the gay people are motivated. If we as, whether you're a Christian or not, if you're just a good conservative, if we were as motivated as the gay people were, the contest would be over. That's just all there is to it. It would be over. But we aren't motivated. I think we've been suckered by this lie of separation of church and state. But there is a new phenomenon going on, has been going on since the last four years in the gay movement, and it's been headed by a gentleman by the name of Tim Gill. He's a software mogul guy who sold his corporation Quark, Q-U-A-R-K, however you say that, he sold it for billions of dollars. He contributed $30 million in '06 to races. He contributed that money to local races, state races and governor races. He gives money, yes, too, on the federal level, but primarily it's on the local level because his philosophy is this: if we're gonna really make changes, we're going to have to do it locally. And what's the saying we always hear and we know, "All politics is local."

And he along with a lot of other gay activists are very disappointed in the national Democratic Party because they've not, you know, they say, they promise all this stuff, you know, we'll acknowledge gays and etc., etc., but when it comes down to really doing policy in Congress, what's always the first to go? The gay agenda stuff because those Democrats, they don't want to alienate their base. So Tim Gill along with a bunch of other people, some other millionaires, billionaires have decided that the way to handle it is on the local level. And they contributed last year over $30 million to state races. They targeted thirteen states. They targeted seventy local politicians. They took out fifty of them. Tim Gill's goal is within ten years to change the face of politics to make it to where there is equality to all people, all lifestyles.

Now, I don't know about you, but the book that I base my life upon is God's Word. And it says to love everybody, and I try to love everybody, but not everybody's lifestyle is equal. Just like not all religions are equal. OK. All money isn't equal. You know, we have this dumb idea now days that tolerance means that everything is equal. Well, everything is not equal. We see that in many areas of our lives. You know, all things are not equal. All religions are not equal.

But, uh, let me just read you some things. Tim Gill along with four other, three other people, let me find this here. I've got so much information, there's no way I can get all of this to you today, but I have it for you to read yourself. Along with a woman by the name of, I think it's Pat Stryker, and then her brother John Stryker...I know I've got them right here, I'll try to fish them out...Pat Stryker, Jared Polis, and Rutt Bridges. They all right now are in Colorado, and they have changed the face of Colorado. For forty years, Colorado's legislature was in the hands of Republicans; in '06, it changed to hands of the Democrats. And the main reason is because they're pushing, these four people, along with other people, and I have a list of them here, the top ones, that you can see.

And this is important because when you start looking at who's contributing to races, say that particular state-wide race we're all concerned about, look for some of these names. They don't give more than $1,000 because they don't want to draw attention, OK, but they will give up to $1,000, and so you start looking for these names. And what they do, their strategy is very under the table, very stealth, and their goal is to find state legislatures that are very tight in their, you know, Republican/Democrat [breakdown], and if just a few races can make the difference to switch it from Republican to Democrat, they're going to target that. And their goal is, in doing that, to intimidate Republicans.

Now the problem we have, I think it's a problem, we've got some moderate Republicans who think it doesn't matter what your lifestyle is, it doesn't matter if you're gay, it doesn't matter if you're for "civil unions," you know. And you notice, the goal is, they're pushing "civil unions" right now. That used to be unheard of, but now that's pretty much acceptable. A lot of Republicans are going for "civil unions," OK. So you know what's going to happen next? Ten years from now, it's going to be gay "marriage." OK, they're taking little by little, they're taking ground little by little, but they're doing it quietly, under the table. They're going into states where the races are close; they're putting in lots of money; and not only that, they're putting people on the ground. Let me read you this. Here this was really, I thought really interesting, I just want to read it. "The key"—this is from a guy by the name of Ted Trimpa, he's kinda like the Karl

Rove for Tim Gill—"the key to success is real grassroots organizing, knocking at the doors, and knock on them again. And don't go turn out the gay vote, go knock on the swing doors as well," he says. "Knock on every door and knock day after day after day."

They took out in Iowa a guy by the name of Danny Carroll, who was the [Republican] Speaker Pro Tem in the House. He thought his race was safe. He lost, a surprise loss. They put people on the ground, young college kids with their iPods going from door to door. Not just Democrats, though, also Republicans, trying to find those swing voters, but they do it time and time again. They say it's expensive and time-consuming, but it is the absolute right way to do real grassroots politics, door to door, talking to the voters, having gay people go to them, allies of ours go to each of them, walk them through, and you flip votes one by one. It's a strategy that works both in the legislature and in the field.

They quote Tim Gill on another aspect of their political strategy. Tim says, "You have to turn down the volume of opponents' 'anti' rhetoric. They can't just say and do everything with license. They have to know beforehand that it's going to cost them some votes and some serious money to play like that. It certainly doesn't stop it, but it turns it way down, and then when they do spew any 'anti' rhetoric, they look extreme. You have to create an environment of fear and respect," said Tim Gill. "The only way to do that is to get aggressive and go out and actually beat them up politically. Sitting there crying and whining about being victims isn't going to get us equality. What is going to get us equality is fighting for it."

What they're trying to do is send a message of

intimidation to those people who are taking a stand for traditional marriage and against the homosexual life-style. They want to silence us, [that] is what they want to do. And it's happening all over the state. You know, the very fact that I'm talking to you like this, here today, puts me in jeopardy. OK, and so, so be it. OK, and I'm not 'anti'; I'm not gay bashing, but according to God's Word, that is not the right kind of lifestyle. It has deadly conse-quences for those people involved in it. They have more suicides, and they're more discouraged; there's more ill-ness; their life spans are shorter. You know, it's not a life-style that is good for this nation.

Matter of fact, studies show that no society that has totally embraced homosexuality has lasted more than, you know, a few decades [I meant to say genera-tions rather than decades]. So it's the death knell for this country. I honestly think it's the biggest threat even that our nation has, even more so than terrorism or Islam, which I think is a big threat, OK. [I meant to say rad-ical Islam]. Because what's happening now, they're going after, in schools, two-year-olds. You know why they're trying to get early childhood education? They want to get our young children into the government schools so they can indoctrinate them. I taught school for close to twenty years, and we're not teaching facts and knowl-edge anymore, folks; we're teaching indoctrination. OK?

We're turning out a citizenry who are learners but not thinkers. By that I mean they take whatever is thrown at them. They don't question it. A thinker listens to what's given to them, and then goes and researches and reasons about it and figures out if this is right or wrong. We aren't developing students like that today. We're developing students who will do whatever the

THE STONING OF SALLY KERN

elites want. That's what we're headed toward, and they're going after our young children as young as two years of age to try to teach them that the homosexual life-style is an acceptable lifestyle. And there are programs they're going after in school. It just, uh, I'm not going to say anymore about that because I have the material over there. You really need to read this article, seven pages, but read it. It has some interesting stuff in it. It will show you their strategy, and we need to be forewarned.

OK, now, where are the social conservative billion-aires? I want to suggest to you that they are few and far between. OK. We've got some, but they don't give money the way the gay philanthropists are giving their money, OK. And, unfortunately, I see a lot of our millionaire conservatives are really bought into big business and even big government, and they don't support social con-servatism. And I think that's a mistake. But in ten years' time our whole landscape, political landscape, could be changed if we don't start giving money, we social con-servatives, people who have it, start giving money to candidates who will stand up for what is right instead of buckling under this. So it's just happening to us right and left.

You know gays are infiltrating city councils. Did you know, Eureka Springs, anybody been there to the Passion Play? Have you heard that the city council of Eureka Springs is now controlled by gays? OK. There are some others: Pittsburgh, Pennsylvania; Tacoma, Maryland; Kensington, Maryland; in Vermont, Oregon, West Palm Beach, Florida; and a lot of other places in Florida. What's happening? The homosexuals are get-ting involved politically on the most local level there is—city council, city government—and they are winning elections, and the first thing they're doing is passing, uh, laws, anti-discrimination laws and hate [crimes] laws and things like that and, uh, you know, one of the things I deal with in our legislature is, I tried to introduce a bill last year that would notify parents, [so] schools [would have] to let parents know what clubs their students were involved in. And the reason I did that bill, primarily, was this: we have the gay/straight alliances coming into our schools.

And we had parents say, "If I knew my child was involved in that group, I wouldn't let them." Kids are getting involved in these groups, their lives are being ruined, [and] their parents don't know about it. So I introduced a bill that said you have to notify [parents of] all clubs and things. And one of my colleagues said, "Well, you know, we don't have a gay problem in my community, and that's why I voted against that bill." Well, you know what? To me that is so dumb. If you got cancer or something in your little toe, do you say, "Well, you know, I'm just going to forget about it because the rest of me is just fine"? It spreads, OK, and this stuff is deadly, and it's spreading, and it will destroy our young people, and it will destroy this nation.

But they're going after city councils; they're influencing schools' sex-ed at schools. Respect for Differences in Human Sexuality is a big sex-ed program they're trying to get into all the schools. And basically what [it] is, it's teaching that you have to be tolerant, you have to accept homosexuality.

This brings in our libraries. OK, you know I believe in the principle as a person thinks, as a man thinks, so is he. That's why we have to be careful about what we read, what we watch, things like that, what music we listen to and stuff because what goes in is what comes out. Garbage in, garbage out. We know that with computers. You know, what you put in is what you get out. OK. You take our young minds and the garbage that they're reading in our libraries, and I mean it's garbage. I should have thought and brought you some excerpts of some of the stuff that, uh, I mean there's no literary value to it at all. It is pure filth. The language, the acts, the things that are going on and yet our kids are reading it, I mean, they are reading [it] in the droves. OK. Kids go home, and I see some high school kids couldn't wait to get out so they could go home and see their favorite soap opera. And I tell them, "Look, that is not real life. They do anything they want and don't suffer consequences. In real life you got consequences."

So, uh, hate crimes, this leads to hate crimes [laws]. If we have hate crimes [laws], our free speech will be silenced. OK. You know I'm not a lawyer, but I think I know enough about this. Law should be dealing with our actions, not with what we are thinking. Nobody can read my mind; nobody can read your mind. OK. If two little old ladies are both murdered, you know, and one's gay and [the] other isn't, why should the one that was gay, [why should] her murderers receive a harsher crime than the ones who murdered the other little old lady? They're both dead. You know, murder is murder. So we've gotta watch; they are coming after these kinds of bills.

Another thing that I'm real big on that is a real detriment to this society is evolution. Evolution undermines Christian principles. Period. That's all there is to it. You either believe there is a Creator, or you believe there isn't. Some people say, "Well, I believe there is a Creator, and He used evolution." There's a lot of problems there, folks.

When does sin come in? When does the spirit come in? You know, it's evolution. You read God's Word, and you will see the word creation all through it, Old and New Testament. And it [the theory of evolution] undermines people's faith. They have trouble reading or believing the Bible.

Choosing Fact Over Fiction

There you have it. That's the speech that changed my life—rushed, rambling, and occasionally poorly worded as it was. So what do you think?

Do you agree or disagree? If you're undecided, let me encourage you to read the next few chapters before you make up your mind. In them I will lay out some of the startling, unreported information that compelled me to start speaking out in the first place. As a wise person once retorted in a debate, "You're entitled to your own opinion, but you're not entitled to your own facts." I will lay out the facts for you, and you may interpret them as you will.

Clearly, those who belong to or are sympathetic to the homosexual activist movement disagreed with what I laid out in my speech. To use some of their own words, they are "disgusted, appalled, outraged" and "can't believe such an ignorant [profanity] still exists today." On the other hand, if you agree with what I said, then perhaps, again in the words of those who have tried to turn my name into a byword, you are a "right-wing, fundamentalist, homophobic, hate-filled bigot who doesn't know the first thing about love."

Let me add that I'm using some of the milder, nicer words that I received to express their opinions of me. Since this is not an X-rated book, I won't use their exact language. In a later chapter I will give some examples of hate e-mail that was sent, but you will have to use your imagination to fill in all the blanks.

Let me first address the "hate" charge that is constantly leveled. It's an accusation any Christian must take seriously. Those who claim the name of Christ are called to be people of love. Just because I oppose the homosexual lifestyle does not mean I hate the people who engage in that behavior. And if it does, why wasn't that same logic applied to Rosie O'Donnell when she said, "Radical Christianity is just as threatening as radical Islam in a country like America"?[1] Was she accused of being a hater of Christians because of what she said?

I hope you can see from reading my speech in its entirety that I was attempting to deal with the homosexual activists' political *agenda*. Webster's dictionary defines *agenda* as "a list or outline of things to do or accomplish." Everyone and every organization has its agenda. Republicans and Democrats have theirs. Education advocates, health care crusaders, the National Rifle Association, and even the media have their agendas, to name just a few groups. Here in America we have that right to have our agendas. We call it freedom.

To pretend that homosexual rights activists don't have an agenda is absurd. Yet among those thousands of e-mails I received in response to two minutes and fifty-nine seconds of my speech that were taken out of context and put on YouTube were many assertions that there is no such thing as a homosexual agenda. Nothing could be further from the truth. If you type "homosexual agenda" or "gay agenda" into an Internet search engine, you'll find information dating back to the 1970s.

Didn't someone once say that if you repeat a lie long enough and loud enough people will eventually come to believe it is true? The claim that there is no homosexual agenda is a classic example of this.

Chapter Three

THE RELUCTANT CANDIDATE

I'M OFTEN ASKED HOW IN THE WORLD A MINISTER'S WIFE became a state representative. After all, everyone knows that religion and politics don't mix. I've heard it said that if you want to ruin a good family reunion, just start talking religion or politics. Speak about both at the same time, and, well, there go peace and fellowship right down the tubes.

Nevertheless, in the Kern household, religion and politics are discussed all the time. Actually, I hope that they are *lived* more than discussed. For my husband and me, religion is more than just a topic. It is the person of Jesus Christ and His way of life as revealed in His Word, the Bible. It's a way of life we sought to teach to our sons with the hope that one day they would choose Jesus as their way of life too.

Some personal history may give you a better understanding of how this pastor's wife became a state legislator and, by the reckoning of at least one homosexual activist, "the most dangerous woman in America."

We've all heard it said that God works in mysterious ways. Boy, do I know that's true. If someone had told me forty years ago that I was going to be a state representative, I would have laughed myself silly. Forty years ago I was a twenty-one-year-old who had her life all mapped out. Being an elected official was not anywhere on my radar. It wasn't even there ten years ago. But then forty years ago I didn't want to get married, have children, be a minister's wife, or be a school-teacher either. I was going to be an old maid missionary. I'm so glad God had a different plan for my life.

More than four decades ago I met Steve Kern. I can still remember the first time I ever saw him. It was at Lake Waxahachie, just outside Waxahachie, Texas, on a Saturday in June 1969. He was getting out of a ski boat standing in ankle-deep water putting on cowboy boots wearing those short swim trunks that were the style back then. In 1969 the term "nerd" wasn't being used, but if there had been such a word then, I most assuredly would have used it to describe the young man I saw. But that first impression was quickly changed when he later took out his guitar and began singing. And it wasn't just any song, but one he had written himself called "Long Way From Eden." That song recounted how far removed from God's original purpose we are today. It is a song that is even more real to me now than it was four decades ago.

I couldn't take this stand if it weren't for the man God brought into my life to be my husband. Would you believe that Steve and I were talking marriage after only two weeks of dating? I'm not one to believe in love at first sight, but that old maid business was gone in no time flat. We were married just seven months after we first met.

God has used Steve to change my life in many ways—first, to show me what it really meant to be a Christian. As I said earlier, I was a very religious and moral person. In the words of the old Texas saying, I didn't "smoke, drink, curse or chew, or go with boys who do." I read the New Testament through every month, and I read the entire Bible through almost every year. But I was missing the key ele-ment that defines what it means to be a Christian—spiritual rebirth and the living, dynamic relationship with God through Jesus Christ that makes it possible.

Over time, Steve showed me what it meant to be submissive to God. I was a very strong-willed person who had deliberately trained myself to always be in control. I felt that was needed if I was going to be a missionary. Steve showed me how to be submissive to God through the life that he lived. The night I finally surrendered to God and accepted His work on the cross for my sins instead of my religious works, I saw my husband in a whole new light. The first few years of our marriage I thought he was timid and too often weak, when actually he just had a humble and meek spirit before the Lord.

It was Steve who suggested I go into teaching, a profession I dearly loved and worked in until I was elected to the state House of Representatives in November 2004. And guess where the suggestion that I run for office came from?

We moved to Oklahoma City, Oklahoma, in March 1996 when the people of Olivet Baptist Church called Steve to be their pastor. I immediately began applying for a teaching position in the local school districts. I ultimately got a job teaching government in a big inner-city high school just two days before the start of school. I'd never taught in a large inner-city high school before, and I think I received more of an education the first couple of years than my students did. But I loved them and wanted to help them become all they were created to be.

A STEP OF FAITH

One day Steve came home and told me he had been invited to be the chaplain of the week for the Oklahoma State House. He had never done anything like this before, and we were both excited about the opportunity. Little did we know what effect his being chaplain of the week would have on our lives.

At some point during that week he said to me, "You should run for office. I've met some of those guys, and you could do that job." I remember looking at him, laughing all the while, and saying, "You must be kidding. I have absolutely no desire to do anything like that." And I didn't. I was thoroughly happy being a minister's wife and a schoolteacher. I loved my job teaching young people. I felt I was making a positive impact on their lives. Plus, I was the girls' golf coach. This meant that I was able to be on the golf course every day, and if you're a golf enthusiast, you know what a big plus this is. Besides, I had summers off to play golf! No, with all this going for me, I had no desire to serve in the state legislature. I told my husband he was crazy for even thinking about it.

In each of the next two years Steve was again asked to serve as chaplain of the week for the state Senate. And on both occasions he again mentioned I should consider running for office, especially since I had taught government for years. And each time I would give him the same answer: "No thanks. Not interested."

Two more years went by without Steve being asked to serve as chaplain, and I thought for sure that was the end of his ridiculous idea. But then there came that day in my government class when the lesson was on campaigns. The discussion was about who runs for office and the money involved. Unfortunately, I found that the prevailing attitude of my students was that only crooked people who are rich and in it for the money run for office. I found myself telling them that they were stereotyping politicians and that while some were crooked and rich and concerned only about money, not all were. Then I made a statement that haunted me for several months and that I'll never forget. I said, "One of these days Mrs. Kern may run for office, and I hope you know that I'm not rich. After all, I'm just a minister's wife and a schoolteacher, and neither of those professions pays lots of money. And I hope you know I'm a person of integrity."

Later that day while sitting in my favorite chair in my family room waiting for Steve to come home, I thought to myself, "Why in the world did you make that statement about maybe someday running for office?" You know how a thought or idea gets in your mind and just won't go away? As hard as I would try, I could not get that thought out of my mind. And I never once mentioned to Steve what I had said to my class or that such a thought was stuck in my mind like a flashing neon sign. I just silently wrestled with it, hoping it would eventually go away.

But it didn't. After inwardly struggling with the idea of running for office, I finally decided to pray about it. Of course, that's something you'd think a minister's wife would decide to do up front. I didn't because I was afraid the Lord might actually *want* me to run. So I began to lift up to the Lord this very hesitant and reluctant prayer, just between God and me. I in no way wanted Steve to know about this. I felt he had forgotten his silly notion, and I was intent on praying it away. But the more I prayed, the more I felt God wanted me to run. This is when I did a very un-Christian-like thing. I flatly said, "No, Lord. I do not want to do this."

You see, I was very content in my role as a minister's wife and a teacher. I was comfortable, and life was good and fairly predictable and easy. I knew that running for an elected office would turn my world upside down and get me out of my comfort zone. Of course, I had no inkling as to how uncomfortable it would ultimately become.

One thing I did know—I was miserable. You can't go against God's will and expect to have peace. So, in time, I finally surrendered.

Once again I was sitting in my favorite chair in our family room waiting on Steve to come home so I could share all of this with him. When he came into the room, the first thing I said to him was, "I'm running." He stopped, looked at me with a puzzled look, and said, "Running for what?" So I cautiously told him of my statement to my class, of the ensuing struggle, and that I now felt God wanted me to run for the office of state representative. I say cautiously because there was a part of me that was hoping he would say he no longer thought it was a good idea for me to run. Then I could be a submissive wife like the Bible talks about and continue teaching with a clear conscience. But he didn't say that. Instead, he gave me two thumbs up and said, "Awesome! I know just the person you need to talk to."

So there I was, stepping out in faith into totally uncharted waters—waters that I suspected would be way over my head. I had been hoping that at the ripe old age of fifty-eight I wouldn't have to step out into the deep anymore. But God had other plans.

Even though I had taught government for almost twenty years and understood the facts about the process and institutions, I knew that my knowledge was all theory. Other than consistently exercising my right and duty to vote, I didn't know anything about the practical side of politics. As a minister's wife serving in my church and being a teacher who taught advanced placement classes as well as coaching, I'd never had any spare time to actually get involved in the day-to-day nuts and bolts of politics. I had never, and I mean *never*, attended a precinct meeting, district meeting, or state political convention. I hadn't even been to the Oklahoma State Capitol. I've since learned that most people who run for office are recruited by party activists. When they heard that Sally Kern was running for House District 84, the response of those insiders was, "Sally who?"

I was way out of my comfort zone and having to depend upon the Lord with a renewed fervency. I was like a driver who thinks she's wide awake behind the wheel, only to have that bumped curb cause her to jerk the steering wheel and bring her back to total awareness where she should have been all along. Well, God had my complete and total attention now.

Nothing to Lose

That person Steve wanted me to talk to was Kay Dudley, a former Oklahoma state senator and Governor Frank Keating's appointment secretary. She was the grand dame of Oklahoma Republican politics. At five feet one inch, she was dynamite in a compressed package but a giant of a Christian. We met for lunch and talked for more than three hours. I instantly felt a oneness with this godly lady. She gave me wonderful advice. She never took any pay and always jokingly reminded me that I was getting what I paid for. In reality, there was no way I could have paid her what she was worth. One of the first nuggets of wisdom she gave me was that although I felt God wanted me to run, that didn't mean I would win.

I was so glad to hear those words! I didn't want to win. I wasn't running to win. I was running to be obedient. I honestly thought that I would run and lose and be a much better government teacher for having had the experience of running. Looking back on this now, I can see God's wisdom through all of this. Since I didn't want to win the election, I had total freedom to tell the voters exactly where I stood on the issues. If they didn't like my positions, then they wouldn't vote for me. I could then continue working at a job I thoroughly loved and do it with a newfound appreciation and a clear conscience. Sounded like a win-win situation to me.

Oklahoma's new term limits law was just kicking in with this election, which meant that anyone who had an interest in running filed for the open seats. There were five individuals who filed for the seat in my home district. I was the darkest dark horse of the bunch. No one in Oklahoma politics had a clue as to who I was. They didn't know me, and I didn't know them. My campaign team was my Sunday school class and other members of our church who came along for the fun of it. None of us had ever done anything like this before. We would meet in my kitchen and dining room and have the best time addressing and stuffing envelopes or whatever else needed to be done. We had a unique, fun-filled adventure that to this day we still laugh about. We were a bunch of nobodies who knew nothing about running a campaign.

I came in first in the primary with 31 percent of the vote. My predecessor's wife, who threw her hat into the ring only five months before the election, came in second with 25 percent of the vote. I felt sure she would come out on top in the runoff as she had name recognition.

There's a little secret I have to let you in on at this point. Something had changed in my heart during that first stage of the primary. I found I wanted to win! I had now invested almost two years of my life in this vision, plus I had taken up all my husband's spare time (like ministers have lots of that!) with campaigning, studying issues, going to all those meetings, and personally knocking three times on thousands of voters' doors. I had come to believe that I was the best candidate for the position. Compared to my two years, my opponent had been working only five months. Still, she came in second. Privately, I still suspected she was going to win. But now I didn't want her to!

The runoff results were 60 percent to 40 percent in my favor. I had won the primary. I was now the Republican candidate running against the Democratic challenger. A Republican had held this seat for the past twenty-four years, and everyone assured me I was home free. Still, I didn't want to be the one to lose the seat to the other party, so I continued working hard up until Election Day. When the final tally was given, I had won with 68 percent of the vote.

Naïve me, I thought the hard part was over. As a minister's wife I had lived in a fishbowl along with the rest of the family. All ministers and their families do. You get used to it and adjust, or you get out of the ministry. I had absolutely no idea that I was going from a fishbowl into a worldwide aquarium.

Chapter Four

THE RAGING FIRESTORMS

THIS IS THE CHAPTER WHERE I NEED YOU TO PARTICIPATE. When I ask a question, mentally answer yes or no. Don't take this little exercise lightly, because you never know when you may have to confront these questions yourself. If you really want to get just a glimpse of what's been happening since my YouTube experience, attempt to answer these questions as honestly as you can, all the while trying to experience the emotions one would have in these situations.

OK. Here are the questions:

- Would you like being belittled every day? Or mocked?

- Would you find pleasure in being told you're an idiot?

- Would you enjoy being called vulgar names?

- Would you like having horrible lies floating over the Internet about your son? Or husband?

- Would you like being threatened with physical harm?

- Would you delight in having to screen all your phone calls because some wacko may be on the other end vomiting profanities at you?

- Would you relish routinely being followed home by the highway patrol to ensure you get there safely?

- Would you like being ridiculed just for taking the Bible for what it says?

- Would you find satisfaction in opening your mail and seeing a page with only four-letter words on it?

- Would you like being called a bigot because you're a Christian?

Now imagine dealing with these circumstances several times a day, every day, for years…having those thoughts in the back of your mind every waking hour and knowing that it isn't going to end any time soon, if ever. Yes, I know the Bible teaches that we are to count it all joy when we face trials. I thank God for that verse and many others like it. I've claimed them countless times each day. But even though a weight lifter knows hoisting those weights repetition after repetition produces a strong, sculpted body, he agonizes and sometimes dreads the workout. At times his body feels like he can't lift that bar one more time. His mind knows the workout is good for him, but his body still has to endure the struggle.

The Bible says it like this: "The spirit is willing, but the flesh is weak" (Matt. 26:41). I do rejoice and am humbled that God would love me so much He'd allow me to lift up His holiness and proclaim the truth of His Word. And His grace has been sufficient. If I had to choose just one verse out of the Bible that I *know* from experience is true, it would be 2 Corinthians 12:9: "My grace is sufficient for you, for power is perfected in weakness."

At times the weight of this experience starts to overcome me only because it is so constant. But every time I cry out to God for His strength and peace, He answers. I've never been more aware of His presence in my life. And that, my friends, is what makes this journey worth it. I have no hate or anger toward anyone who has attacked me, and that's only because of God's grace.

What I hope to do now is show you the kinds of attacks my family and I have experienced since coming to the attention of the nation's online homosexual network. Keep in mind that I will never be able to adequately express the emotions we've dealt with. Steve's and my life have forever been changed. Things are different. Just like Dorothy said to Toto in *The Wizard of Oz*, "We aren't in Kansas anymore." We hadn't left Oklahoma, but things were drastically different.

It was the Gay and Lesbian Victory Fund that released on YouTube a portion of my speech. Since the speech was just audio, they added pictures of people holding up signs that said, "We're listening." That video has had more than a million hits. Their video spawned many others. At one count there were more than forty YouTube videos dealing with me in derogatory and insulting ways. Only two have been found that are supportive.

Some of these videos were put to jazz, rap, or country music. There was one called "Bashing Gays Again" set to the tune of "On the Road Again." The first few lines go like this:

> Bashing gays again.
> Sally Kern can't wait to start bashing gays again.
> A life she loves is bashing gays with her sick friends.
> Sally Kern can't wait to start bashing gays again.

It's funny in a pathetic sort of way. But notice that anyone who agrees that the homosexual lifestyle is contrary to God's natural order is "sick."

Other videos were poems. One even equates me with Nazi Germany, complete with a German voice reminiscent of Hitler's that starts speaking and then fades away. I have to give it to whoever wrote this poem: it's very creative. But it displays an attitude of mocking not only me but also God. The Bible teaches that there is sinful behavior, and it has consequences not just for individuals but society as a whole. But then again, to understand this, you have to believe in sin.

Then there were other YouTube videos that were parodies, caricatures, impersonations of me, or just people spouting off. What you have to keep in mind with all of these is that there were usually very offensive pictures being displayed while the video was playing. One impersonation ended with the individual appearing to be eating a dog. It was gross to say the least. All of them are intended to demean, insult, and ridicule me and to make me look like a fool.

Once the Victory Fund's video was out on YouTube, the onslaught of hate e-mail began to hit my capitol e-mail account. Within a week almost thirty thousand e-mails had been sent. The volume was so great that the capitol server nearly shut down. We're talking about a statewide entity that has sophisticated software security and is used to getting thousands of e-mail messages on a regular basis. Even the IT people at the capitol hadn't seen anything like this.

Most of those initial e-mails were extremely hateful. It took awhile for those who agreed with my stance to start expressing their support. Unfortunately, that is the way it usually is. Surveys consistently show that the vast majority of Americans oppose radical homosexual activism, and yet that majority remains a silent one. Could that be because they simply don't want to have to deal with the hate and scorn that will come their way? Somehow I don't think being silent is what

Jesus had in mind when He called us to be salt and light in our world. I know we don't always have to be vocal in order to be a witness. But there comes a time when we have to speak up. We must live our faith and speak it as well.

E-MAILING HATE

Below are some examples of the type of e-mails I received. Of course, I'm not going to include the profane and vulgar words. You'll just have to use your imagination, and I apologize for encouraging you to do that. I just want to give you a feel of what came my way. It was not pleasant to read, and, since the battleground for the Christian is in the mind, reading this stuff really tore me up. You won't get the full effect of the e-mails since I've not quoted the profane and vile language. But maybe you can get just a taste of what was dished out to me.

The Bible tells us that Christians have an enemy, and his name is Satan. His job is to condemn us. He sought to use these e-mails to discourage me, defeat me, and make me feel worthless. It was a daily struggle of epic proportions to continually practice the truth of 2 Corinthians 10:5: "taking every thought captive to the obedience of Christ." But that struggle has made me stronger in my faith.

All of these quotes are shown just as they were received. No changes have been made in spelling or grammar. Only the names have been left off and the profanity omitted. Some are from that first week, while others are more recent.

> You are the [profanity] devil for spreading lies and HATE! SHAME ON YOU HILLBILLY [profanity]!!

Dear Sally, you are such a dumb [profanity]!!!! I DO KNOW YOY WILL ROTT IN HELL, AS YOU DESERVE GOD WILL PUNNISH YOU, YOU DIRTY [profanity].

I am in no way threatening you, please know this. I just believe in the power of prayer, and I pray that you get gang-[profanity] in the [profanity], you ignorant [profanity]. My prayers are with you.

YOU IGNORANT BIGOTED [profanity]!!!!! YOU have no right to say no to gay marriage. It is only fair for Gays to have the same rights as you bigoted, ignorant [profanity] holds. YOU ARE nothings but a bullying [profanity]....You and the Mormon supporters who voted for PROP 8 are the polygamist abusers of marriage, not gays....SO GO [profanity] YOURSELF YOU WICKED [profanity] I WISH THE WORST CANCER on you, and the most horrible DEATH I can imagine....POX ON YOU AND YOUR ENTIRE FAMILY

SALLY: ARE YOU A LESBIAN? CAUSE YOU SURE DO LOOK LIKE ONE! MUST BE THE SHORT HAIR AND MUSTACHE. (A little bleach will take care of that - the mustache, I mean.) If you set your hair on fire, it will probably take care of the rest of you! Then you can BURN IN HELL, you poor excuse for a human!

I heard what you said and you should be killed you stupid [profanity]! Along with George W. Bush! Christianity is the cancer in our society and should be eliminated!

You're a horrible person who deserves to burn in hell. Go eat ur closeted girlfriends loose old [profanity], stupid [profanity] looking like a cheep crack whore.

Go [profanity] some [profanity] for money or friends
WHORE [profanity] you stupid dyke

What the [profanity] is your problem??? Were you
dropped on your head as an infant or are all republicans
as mentally retarded as you obviously are??? You homophobic buttkiss. READ THE CONSTITUTION YOU
NAZI FREAK!!!! HELLO!!! 14th amendment is calling,
READ IT YOU MORON!!!!!!!!!!!!!!!!!!!!

First of all, Let me start by saying, I am thrilled to
know that you are being outed publicly for your wrong
doing, and closed minded state of mind. You're a dis-
gusting human being, and you will receive no respect,
from the state of Oklahoma. I am truly ashamed that
a closed minded piece of garbage like yourself represents Oklahoma. Realize that one day, Gay's will domi-
nate this world. Which will be a blessing, because there
will be more peace, justice, and less of pig's like yourself.
Please, go kill yourself.

YOU ARE A HOMOPHOBIC [profanity] YOU [pro-
fanity] DIE

No doubt you get the picture. Just remember that, as of this
writing, there have been more than thirty thousand of these types
of e-mails. Those personal attacks, although not easy to read, at least
focused on me for my remarks. I could understand their lashing out
at *me*. But the messages that came attacking my son and husband
were especially difficult to deal with. They reveal the intense hate and
anger directed toward those who reject the homosexual lifestyle. It's
just a fact of human nature that we lash out at those who we think
have hurt us.

What's really sad is that they truly believe that if their lifestyle is accepted and mainstreamed, they will have peace. Since God made us in His image, and since He is holy and Scripture says in 1 Peter 1:16 that we are to be holy as He is holy, none of us will have peace until we accept what God's standards are. And I'm as much a sinner as anyone else. As the saying goes, "But for the grace of God, there go I."

I'm going to give only a few examples of the ugly and hateful e-mails that slandered my son and husband, although I could give countless additional ones:

> Guess what I just found out? Sally Kern's son Jesse was arrested in Shawnee for sodomy back in 1988. Isn't this a hoot? I even hear that homophobic hating Sally and her husband have disowned him. Real "Christian" of them.

> I read that your son Jesse may be gay and that you and your husband have disowned him. I could not help but think how hurtful your comments must have been for your son to hear. It will be very difficult to sit across from your son at the dinner table if he comes home for Easter. I'm sure that Jesus would prefer to have dinner with Jesse and his friends than you or "churched" friends. Jesus questioned the church, it's leaders and challenged us to be our brother's keeper. God is all about love. Love is sacred and should be honored wherever it is found as it is precious whether it be between a man and a woman, a woman and another woman, a man and another man or a person and some part of nature, art or science.

> Not only is Rep Kern's son gay but her husband was a member of the KKK when they lived in Boise, ID. Yep, the model example of a great Christian family.

Someone obviously took the time to try and dig up information on my family. Too bad they didn't take the time to find out if what they came up with was true or not. In 1988 in Shawnee, Oklahoma, there was an individual named Jesse Jacob Kern who was arrested as an adult for sodomy. My son's name is Jesse Aaron Kern. In 1988 he was twelve years old, and we lived in Boise, Idaho. The fact that my son was not arrested, and has never been arrested, for sodomy or anything else doesn't seem to matter. The lie is out in cyberspace, and the homosexual community continues to spread it to this day. Jesse has to live with it for the rest of his life.

For the seven years we lived in Boise, Idaho, Steve was the pastor of Calvary Baptist Church. It was a wonderful experience, and we still have many dear friends up in the Northwest. I encourage anyone to take the time to contact this church and our friends up there. They will find that there is absolutely no evidence of Steve having ever been a member of the KKK while there or anywhere else for that matter.

A Campaign of Harassment

To this day I continue to get numerous hateful e-mail messages each week. E-mail is easy to ignore, of course. The delete button makes them disappear. But the defiling attacks didn't stop with e-mail. Some of these same individuals also signed me up for every kind of homosexual electronic newsletter there is. When I tried to unsubscribe, a message came back saying, "No such e-mail address was found." So I continue to get them. One such newsletter displayed a deeply offensive picture on my computer screen. When I attempted to delete it, it "hijacked" my computer's browser software and infected it with a Trojan horse virus. I had to call in a technician to remove it and restore my computer. Needless to say, I just keep deleting. Delete. Delete. Delete.

I also mysteriously started getting regular mail and publications that arrived in brown paper coverings. Not only had they signed me up for electronic newsletters, but they also subscribed me to major homosexual magazines and pornography. When the bills began arriving, I just wrote "cancel" across them and sent them back. I've often wondered what my mailman thought about me as he delivered those to my house.

One day I got an e-mail from my webmaster saying he wanted to join my MySpace network. I replied saying I had no MySpace page. Guess what? Someone had created one for me. It had all my personal information, several pictures of me, and a couple of links to news channel interviews. When it first came up, nice Christian music started playing, and there was a background of crosses. At first blush it seemed authentically mine. But as you examined it further, it became obvious that it was intended to make me look like some religious kook. It took some doing, but we finally got it removed.

This kind of antagonism, though hurtful, was not surprising. Christianity is the major cultural obstacle between radical homosexual activists and their goal, which is not mere acceptance or tolerance but *endorsement*. Homosexual activist John Corvino confirmed this when, regarding the gay marriage controversy, he wrote:

> Gay people don't want merely to be tolerated or accepted, we want to be embraced and encouraged—like everyone else in society.... We are not simply asking people to "tolerate" something we do "in the privacy of our bedrooms." We are asking them to support and encourage something we do publicly. We are asking them, in effect, to participate.[1]

Did you really notice what Corvino was saying? It isn't truly tolerance the radical homosexual activists want. They want everyone to morally validate their behavior as healthy and appropriate. Think about that.

There were other elements in the campaign of harassment against us. For a while it seemed that each new week brought a new and unexpected outrage. For example, someone essentially stole my name—registering the "dot com" web address connected to my name—and built a bogus Sally Kern website. Any unsuspecting visitor to the site is greeted by a picture of me, my name in bold letters, followed by the words, "Bashing Gays for Jesus." The introductory text is an adolescent blend of mockery and blasphemy:

> Sally Kern is an Oklahoma State Representative who belongs to the Party of Jesus, formerly known as the Republican Party. Since Jesus has selected the Party of Jesus as his official political party, all dogma revealed by Party of Jesus legislators is inspired directly by Jaheezus. It's official!

You don't have to be a rocket scientist to get the point that both Jesus and Sally are the butt of the joke here. It's one thing to have your purse or some other personal item stolen, but your name? You can easily replace things, but your name is something very personal. Now and for many years to come, any time someone googles my name, my reputation will be further smeared and my character once again slandered.

The home page for this fake Sally Kern site provides links to other affiliated sites, with names like Jesus Wafers, No God Blog, Ain't No God, Atheism Rocks, Atheist Fag, Freedom From Religion, God Not Found, Imaginary Bearded Sky Daddy, Jaheezus, Planet Atheism, and many others. On these sites you'll see Christians called the "religious fundie faction." Meanwhile, the Bible is referred to as "an ancient fairy tale book" whose teachings are "ancient superstitions based on sociopathic rants of genocidal warring tribes."

I could go on and on giving examples of intimidation tactics hurled my way. For instance, five weeks in a row one of Oklahoma's leading homosexual activists attended our church. He would come and sit in the back and take notes like crazy. I told Steve to just send him the sermon tapes. That way he would have no excuse for misrepresenting any statements Steve made. Finally he quit coming. Our entire church was praying for him. When he came, he heard the truth of God's Word. Steve and I pray regularly for that man that God would take what he heard and use it to transform his life.

Then there was the onslaught of letters and e-mail sent to the other legislators and even the governor demanding that they force me to resign or that they reprimand me. The secretary for the Speaker of the House told me that for several days it was almost impossible to do any work because of all the phone calls demanding that the speaker take some action against me. I was thankful that the speaker did not cave in to the pressure. Actions such as these toward me and my colleagues, if coming from any other group, would be considered harassment, but even without hate crimes laws, these activists seemed to have a protected status. As long as hate crimes laws are on the books, they will enjoy even more protection.

Manufacturing Controversy

In the months that followed, the initial tsunami of anger and mockery subsided, but relentless waves of attack continued to come. The steady drumbeat of mockery eventually began to have its desired twofold effect: (1) marginalizing critics of the homosexual political agenda and (2) frightening the wavering into silence or surrender.

For example, in April 2008 the *Journal Record* of Oklahoma City, a local business-oriented weekly newspaper, published a story essentially blaming me for the city's *possible* loss of a business relocation deal.

The headline read, "OKC Chamber: Kern Spooks Big Biz Relocation Consultant."[2]

The headline served up a big "I told you so" opportunity to those who think folks like me should just keep quiet about what we believe. But anyone who bothered to dig deeper than the headline would have smelled a clever propaganda ploy. The first paragraph of the piece told readers that Oklahoma City was still being considered for the relocation deal. The article went on to say:

> Tom Maloney, vice president of California-based Staubach Co., would neither confirm nor deny that the 1,000-employee, AAA-rated client company's top executive is a lesbian who expressed concern over Oklahoma Rep. Sally Kern's recent anti-homosexual statements, as has been the topic circulating among local business leaders.[3]

This is classic. The homosexual activist lobby first manufactures a firestorm of controversy over remarks I made to a small group of constituents; then a San Francisco–based company with a homosexual CEO points to that manufactured controversy surrounding little old me as a reason it may not relocate to Oklahoma City; then some business-at-any-cost types at the Chamber of Commerce publicly wring their hands and fret about how I might be damaging the city's image. Of course, the headline and opening paragraphs of the article appeared on the front page above the fold. One of the final paragraphs, buried back on page twenty-three of the paper, points out that no one has actually expressed any concern about my remarks:

> "It [my remarks] did not come up in any of the governor's economic development team meetings with consultants or discussions we've had with consultants," Pratt said.[4]

So in truth, this chilling effect on business I was supposed to be having was all theoretical. This did not stop the *Journal Record* from penning an editorial in July 2009 with the headline "Sally Kern Is Bad for Business."[5]

Ironically, just as the *Journal Record* was publishing its piece on how much I'm hurting my city's business environment, the magazine *Fortune Small Business* was preparing its list of the best major cities in the country to launch a new business. When the magazine came out in October, at the very top of their list was Oklahoma City. The magazine article cited many of the city's virtues:

> Stable and affordable, Oklahoma City is a haven for entrepreneurial risk takers. It boasts the second lowest foreclosure rate among large U.S. metro areas, along with the second lowest median rent. Through the Great Recession this former Dust Bowl capital has been spared many hardships, with a diverse local economy spread across medical research, energy, education and government.[6]

The piece also noted some of the city's drawbacks, the two principal ones being tornadoes and limited client entertainment options such as professional sports games. Oddly enough, nowhere on the list of negatives was the presence of a cookie-baking grandmother-legislator with a stubborn tendency to bring her traditional, biblical values with her to the floor of the state House of Representatives.

Some of these attacks have clearly carried the goal of simply holding me up to public scorn or embarrassment. Others have obviously been aimed at getting me removed from office. One move seems to have been designed to do both. In September 2009, Oklahoma City attorney Brittany Novotny announced her Democratic candidacy for my House seat. Brittany is a transgender individual; that is, she was born a boy and underwent sex change procedures at some point. I support Brittany's right to run and welcomed the opportunity to openly discuss the issues, but it seems the voters of my conservative district—filled with retirees and working-class families—were not as enthusiastic. I won with 66 percent of the vote.

Although I found all of these attacks overwhelming, almost beyond belief, I continued to remind myself that what was happening was a confrontation between two totally different worldviews. These worldviews are secular humanism and biblical Christianity. This is a spiritual battle. That is why I don't hate those who have maliciously maligned me. Neither does Steve. We pray for them on a regular basis.

Chapter Five

THE TROOPS RALLY

THE BIBLE SAYS IN 1 THESSALONIANS 5:18 TO "GIVE THANKS in everything, for this is God's will for you in Christ Jesus." A sermon I heard almost forty years ago about this verse has had a profound effect upon my thinking, largely shaping my attitude toward life. The preacher pointed out the verse says that *in* all things we are to give thanks. It doesn't say to give thanks *for* all things.

What an awesome truth! In other words, as events happen to us in life that are difficult or tragic, and we all have such times in our lives, God doesn't expect us to be thankful *for* those things. Nobody wants to go through horrible experiences. But even as we go through them, we can be thankful because God is still God, and He is in control. And it's only as we give thanks *in* every trial that we truly express our faith in God.

That's why, even amid all the attacks we were enduring, there was still cause to give thanks. For example, when the local homosexual community in Oklahoma City had their "Shame on Sally" rallies, I gave thanks. Regardless of what was taking place, I was hanging on to the fact that God was in control and thanking Him for that.

There were at least three "Shame on Sally" rallies that the news media covered. God used these rallies to emphasize that this situation was not about me. It's about something much bigger than any one person. It's about our society and where we are morally and whether or not those who believe the truth of God's Word will take a stand.

During this battle, this truth of giving thanks in everything has sustained me every day, many times a day. It's been like a spiritual workout that has resulted in a stronger walk with the Lord. This is why I have no hate in my heart for those who have attacked me. God has used them to draw me closer to Him, and that is a blessing, not a curse. And as good people saw me being condemned and denounced for holding the same values they hold, many rallied to my defense. It was heartening, to say the least.

In order to really grasp the significance of the overwhelming show of encouragement and support given to me, you have to know a little more about those "Shame on Sally" rallies. The first occurred on a Saturday night at a local park. According to newspaper accounts there were about two hundred protesters there along with the media. Another took place near Memorial Park with, again, a crowd of about two hundred present. The media were also there. Protesters had crafted colorful signs of all shapes, sizes, and slogans and proudly displayed them.

On Tuesday, March 18, 2008, the largest rally was held in the rotunda of the Oklahoma State Capitol. *The Oklahoman*, Oklahoma's largest daily newspaper, reported about three hundred people gathered around the state seal.[1] Several speakers addressed the group, all demanding that I apologize or resign from office. "Hateful speech leads to hate crimes just as surely as the sun rises in the morning," said one speaker.[2] Funny, but all the hateful speech directed at me was never mentioned as a precursor to hate crimes. Another speoaker said, "If she does that [apologize], she shows good will and good faith;

if she doesn't, we think she's ignoring us, and we think that what she's done is just deplorable, and she ought to resign as a public person."[3]

Ironically, if I had indeed been "ignoring" the homosexual community, none of this would have ever happened. It seems, in their view, that I'm only ignoring them and doing deplorable things if I don't agree with them.

These rallies received much sympathetic media coverage in the major daily and weekly newspapers and by the network television affiliates. There appeared to be an effort by the media to portray me as an extremist and as way out of step with the opinions of most Oklahomans. This was a huge mistake on their part as it aroused the sleeping giant in Oklahoma, the conservative Christians.

It wasn't that I was so popular or even such a sympathetic figure. The fact was, I was being attacked and condemned for holding views that are held by the vast majority of Christians. These Oklahomans accurately viewed these attacks on me as attacks on themselves as well.

For example, there is an organization called Reclaiming Oklahoma for Christ. For the past three years it has held a conference encouraging God's people to get out of the four walls of the church and get involved in addressing the social issues of our day. These are the very issues that, as we see in the Bible, have plagued societies from the beginning of time. In the Bible, Christians are admonished to be salt and light in the world. And we can't be salt and light if we stay cooped up in our churches.

A "Rally for Sally"

As it happened, the leaders of Reclaiming Oklahoma for Christ had scheduled a planning meeting for their next conference a few days after one of the "Shame on Sally" rallies. As they were discussing the protest rally, someone suggested there should be a "Rally for Sally."

That was all it took. The idea was born, and these men ran with it. Not one of them had any idea how significant this event would grow to be.

It was felt that as many people as possible needed to plan the rally. They decided to call it the "Freedom of Speech Rally for Sally." A call was put out for people to come to a planning meeting held at a local church. To everyone's surprise, fifty-two people showed up. Some were pastors, and others were laypeople all wanting to show their support for a fellow believer. The manager of a local Christian radio station, KQCV, an affiliate in the Bott Radio Network, attended and volunteered to provide the sound system as well as help to publicize the event. Churches across the state were invited to come stand with Sally.

A program was put together that included several speakers. The group decided that I needed to address the crowd at this event as well. I would have been content just being a spectator. My husband, Steve, was also asked to speak briefly and lead the Pledge of Allegiance. The director of First Stone Ministries, a local recovery and support group for those dealing with same-sex attractions, was invited to share his journey out of homosexuality. Pastor Paul Blair, founder of Reclaiming Oklahoma for Christ, would also speak. At the last minute, the president of Americans for Truth About Homosexuality (AFTAH), Peter LaBarbera, flew into town from Illinois and was added to the program. A couple of pastors would voice prayers, and another would lead music. Reid Mullins, the morning talk show host of a local radio station, was enlisted to be the master of ceremonies.

Now all that was left was the praying. Prayers went up asking God to bring people to the capitol on Tuesday, April 2, at noon. Most of all, we were praying that God would be lifted up and glorified.

I had no idea what I would say, but I started praying from the moment I was asked to speak. The legislature was in session at that time, so the days were long. At home in the evenings, after reading bills, I'd ask God for wisdom to know the right thing to say. This went on for more than a week, and nothing was jelling. Nervousness was starting to set in. Finally, the night before the rally, I sat down and began writing. The words just poured out. My talk was only about eight minutes long, but I knew it was what God had given me.

We woke up Tuesday morning to a cold, windy, drizzling wet day. Not a good day to get out if you could stay in.

I was already nervous about this day, but now that the weather was so bad, an onslaught of negative thoughts began to invade my mind:

- "What if there were fewer people at this rally than at the protesters' rallies?"

- "Christians don't brave the weather to go to church on Sundays; they won't get out in this to come to the capitol, especially with so little parking available."

I had to fight hard to reject thoughts like these. "*In* everything give thanks." I had to actively repeat this phrase over and over in my mind. I kissed Steve good-bye and headed off to the capitol for our legislative session at 9:00 a.m. He said he would meet me in my office at 10:30 a.m.

There were many reasons why I was nervous that day. One was because an e-mail had been sent to the office warning us that not everyone present at the rally was going to be supportive. It also said that some of these unfriendly individuals were going to demand that I answer some questions there in front of everybody. The last thing any of us wanted was for this rally to turn into a confrontational spectacle. Would such a thing happen? The possibility of this only added to my apprehension.

Frankly, when I received that e-mail, it made me mad. You see, when the protesters had their rallies, we didn't intrude on their freedom of expression. We respected their right to assemble and make their case. But they were not going to extend us the same courtesy. There was that double standard.

While the legislature is in session, there are always different groups and organizations at the capitol. From the moment you enter the building, you hear the buzz of conversations and are overcome with the tempting aroma of food. It's as if the building itself is alive and pulsating with the activity within its walls. Today seemed especially so. I prayed this was a good sign for the rally.

We were in session on the House floor only about an hour. When I returned to my office, the reception area was teeming with people. Some were familiar, but others were just dropping by to wish me well, saying they were praying for me. Peter LaBarbera was sitting in my office reading. Soon Nate, our second son, showed up. It meant a lot to me that he would take time off from work to support his mother. Finally, Steve arrived with news that California pastor Wiley Drake was going to be calling any minute to interview me on his Internet radio show. What I really wanted to do was just be alone, sit still, and let God calm my spirit. But being alone and quiet was out of the question.

The next thing we knew a capitol police officer rushed into the office needing to talk to us. He seemed a little frantic, and we had no idea what was wrong.

He asked if it were possible to move the rally outside on the south steps of the capitol. Seems that the crowd was so large, security would have to turn people away. The first floor rotunda and each ancillary wing were filled with people jammed together. As he expressed his concerns, we realized this was a good problem to have. Security had already routed hundreds of people to the second and third floors. He estimated that approximately two thousand people were currently in the capitol, with at least a thousand more waiting to get in.

I could hardly believe what he was saying. The news of a crowd this large overwhelmed me. I was literally stunned. The magnitude of what was about to take place was more than I could comprehend. I remember just thanking God for His goodness and asking for His grace.

It was decided that at this point in time, it was not feasible to move everything and relocate outside. Also, the weather was not conducive to having the rally outdoors. The rally would go on as planned.

While this discussion was going on, the phone call from Pastor Wiley Drake in California came through. As we talked, he said the rally would be carried live via the Internet around the world on the *Wiley Drake Show*. All I could think about was that verse in 1 Corinthians 2:9: "What no eye has seen and no ear has heard, and what has never come into a man's heart, is what God has prepared for those who love Him."

Finally it was time to go downstairs. There in the reception area of my office, Steve; Nate; TJ, my legislative assistant; Kristin, my intern; Peter LaBarbara; and Bill Snelson, a constituent; and I joined hands and prayed. Then two capitol police officers came to escort us to the first floor.

It felt strange being escorted through the halls and down the stairs with a police officer in front and one behind. As we went, people would shout out, "God bless you, Sally," or "You're in our prayers." I was overwhelmed and still a little nervous.

"Courageous," "Brave," "Hero"?

When we arrived on the first floor on the west side of the rotunda, we had to push our way through the crowd to get to the podium. People began chanting, "Sal-lee, Sal-lee, Sal-lee." The echo rang throughout the corridors of the capitol. I was overcome with emotion and had to fight back the tears. "God, is this really happening?" I thought to myself. This grandmother who'd rather go unnoticed was about to step before the largest gathering she'd ever faced. I was extremely humbled. And after the many weeks of verbal abuse via every available medium, the support was like a healing balm. But I'd never asked for anything like this. This was definitely a God thing.

The rally started off on a humorous note as Reid Mullins, the emcee, said, "Sally Kern is a woman who proves the slogan, 'A woman's place is in the House.'" After welcoming everyone, he introduced my husband with these words, "Behind every great woman is a pretty good man." I thought to myself, "If anyone in the Kern household approaches greatness, it's Steve, not me," and I thanked God that I had a man like him.

Steve's role in the rally was twofold. First, he was to lead in the flag salute, and then he was to introduce me. However, after leading the Pledge of Allegiance, he took the opportunity to say a few words:

> We're not here today to bash homosexuals. We love them. Nor are we here to ask for any apology or anyone's resignation for all the thousands of hate mail or the national Internet defamation and denigration of our son, Jesse Aaron Kern. We want to say to all of those who passed those lies along that we forgive you. We have no animosity in our heart against you. We pray God's forgiveness on you.

He then prayed and introduced me by saying, "Ladies and gentlemen, let me introduce to you my wife and helpmate for thirty-eight years, from the great state of Oklahoma and District 84, state representative and foremost KERNservative, Sally Kern." The crowd erupted into cheers, and those fortunate enough to have chairs stood up.

As I approached the podium, there were many emotions running through my body. It took a little while to get the crowd quiet, and then I began my speech.

> I want to thank you so much for being here today. I can't tell you how much this means to me, and, yes, *wow* is an awesome word to describe it. This rally, "Freedom of Speech Rally for Sally," is really about freedom of speech for all of us who want to stand up for the truth of God's Word. Ladies and gentlemen, I want you to know, I know this is not about me. This is not about me. It's about the church having the right to speak out about the redeeming love of Jesus Christ, who died to set us all free from our sin.

> Since this has been happening, I've really, I mean, I read my Bible all the time anyway, but I've really been in the Scripture, and God gave me a verse right after this happened. It's Philippians 1:12, where the apostle Paul says, "I want you to know that what has happened to me has served to the advancement of the gospel," and that's the way I'm looking at this. To God be the glory.

> I've gotten lots of e-mails lately, to put it mildly. Some have been good, and for those of you that have sent good ones, I thank you for them. I appreciate it. Some have not been so good. I've been called lots of names, and I can't repeat most of those names. Some of the good names that I've been called have been "courageous," "brave," and "a hero." I want you to know, and I mean this with all my heart, I have more trouble relating to those good names than I do the bad names.

> I say that because I know I'm a sinner, and I'm not worthy of God's grace. And I know, also, that I'm not courageous, I'm not brave, and I'm certainly not a hero. I'm just an earthen vessel, an old clay pot, the way

2 Corinthians 4:7 says, "We have this treasure in earthen vessels, clay jars, to show that this surpassing power is from God." So the last few weeks have been pretty tough. I have to be honest. But God's grace has been sufficient. So if I seem courageous, if I seem brave, if I seem like a hero, I want you to know it's God's grace, and to Him be the glory.

When I gave that infamous speech, I was not putting down any individuals. I believe each and every person is created in God's image and is precious in His sight. He loves all of us. He loves all of us equally, and He loves all of us regardless of what our sin is. Yet God is not just a God of love. He is also a righteous and holy God who sent His Son to die for our sins so that we could have forgiveness and experience life abundantly. But to have His forgiveness, we must first acknowledge our sin. We can't excuse it, and we can't try to justify it.

Let me tell you why I will not and why I cannot apologize for my comments. First, I believe God's Word. When God calls something a sin, then that settles it. It is a sin. God never changes. He says He's the same yesterday, today, and forever, and His Word never changes. My opinion doesn't matter. What matters is God's Word.

Second, this nation was founded on Christian principles. Some will try to say that's not the case, but they need to read the primary sources of our Founding Fathers. We all know Patrick Henry's famous words, "Give me liberty or give me death," but do you know he also said, "It cannot be emphasized too strongly or too often that this great nation was founded not by religionists but by Christians. Not on religions but on the gospel of Jesus Christ."

Some say that we should separate church and state.

God never intended to separate the influence of our faith from the institutions of government. He wanted to separate the institutions. He didn't want the church controlling the state. Nor did He want the state controlling the church. But you cannot separate your faith from life. Christians can't do that.

Noah Webster, the same Noah Webster who wrote the dictionary back in 1828, said these words when he was writing to schoolchildren. He said, "When you become entitled to exercise the right of voting for public officers, let it be impressed on your mind that God commands you to choose for rulers just [or righteous] men who will rule in the fear of God." I believe these words.

The third reason that I cannot apologize is because I told the people when running for this office that I was a Christian candidate and that I believed we were in a cultural war for the very existence of our Judeo-Christian values. This situation proves that I was right. We are in a cultural war. It is real. This situation gives me the opportunity to keep my promise to those who voted for me, and that's what I'm doing.

Psalm 11:3 says this, "When the foundations are being destroyed, what can the righteous do?" We can remember that the foundation of society is the home as established by God—one man and one woman. We can remember that the foundation of this nation was Christianity. So teach it to our children. We can remember that the foundation of the church is God's Word. So believe it and practice it every day. We can remember that the foundation of salvation is Christ dying for a lost world in bondage to sin. Proclaim the truth that will set people free.

When you go home today, I'd like to ask you to do

something. Go turn all the lights on in your bedroom and then get in the closet. Make sure there are no lights on there. Stand there in the dark for a few minutes and then open the closet door and notice what happens. You're going to see that the darkness does not swoop out of the closet and overtake the light. No, folks, the light spreads to the closet, dispelling the darkness. Our world is dark with sin today not because of the homosexuals, not because of the murderers or drug addicts or anybody else we would name. It's dark because the church, you and me, have not let our light shine.

So what can we, the righteous, do to shore up the foundations? We need to pray with all of our hearts 2 Chronicles 7:14: "If My people, who are called by My name, will humble themselves and pray and seek My face and turn from their wicked ways, then will I hear from heaven and will heal their land."

Thank God that we still have freedom of speech in America. Let's speak while we still can. God bless you, and God bless America.

The speech wasn't delivered eloquently. Some words were stumbled over. Even Bible verses were misquoted. But God was there. I felt like God my Father had reached down and hugged His child that day. God used that rally to humble me but also to encourage and embolden me anew.

Stephen Black spoke next. Stephen is the director of First Stone Ministries, a ministry to those who are dealing with homosexuality and other sexual sins. He shared how he had been molested twice as a young boy and how this had deeply scarred his image of men, especially since his relationship with his father was poor. He briefly told how a friend introduced him to the homosexual community, and he said the eight years he lived that lifestyle were the darkest of his life. Then he recounted how God revealed Himself to him and set him free from the bondage of sin, which also released him from the clutches of homosexuality.[4]

Following Stephen was Peter LaBarbara, who announced to the people that leaders and organizations of pro-family groups from all across America were standing with me in this battle for traditional marriage. He had personally contacted more than ninety such groups who gave their support.

Last to speak was Pastor Paul Blair. Pastor Paul was an All-American lineman on the Oklahoma State University football team who went on to play with the Chicago Bears. Needless to say, he is a big man, and he has a compassionate heart to match his stature. He closed out the rally recalling some of America's godly heritage. He finished by challenging all listening to "stand with me and to stand with Governor Sally Kern."

"Governor Sally Kern?" I thought to myself, "Did he really say that?" As I was being whisked away by security, a microphone was shoved into my face and a reporter asked if I thought I'd run for governor. "No," I said. "I'm honored to serve as a state representative, and God has me right where He wants me."

Scripture says, "This is the day the LORD has made; let us rejoice and be glad in it" (Ps. 118:24). A lot of rejoicing and gladness takes place whenever the "Freedom of Speech Rally for Sally" is talked about in our home. It was a unique day that blessed our hearts and will forever have a special place in our memories. Nate, our youngest son, was able to attend the rally and had this to say about it.

> Some moments in life are surreal. They leave you asking yourself, "Did that really happen, or is this some kind of dream?" This moment was like that. Let me begin with

a little context, though. Our family is pretty normal. Outsiders would not look at us and think we were of much importance in the world. My dad's been a preacher in a few humble churches pretty much all of my life, and my mom's a schoolteacher. Was a schoolteacher, I should say. We've never been rich, monetarily speaking, and still aren't. We've never been insiders or power grabbers. My mom began her political career in her upper fifties with zero name recognition and little expectation of victory. Somehow a hotly contested race left her the last person standing.

Speaking of surreal, that in itself was pretty surreal. Suddenly, four years later, there we were in her office waiting for the rally. A radio host speaking to my dad asks if he can talk to me about the goings on, a request I decline. Honestly, everything was crescendoing into a little more publicity than I would ever care for. My mother probably felt the same way. She certainly never expected or wanted all of this. The next thing I know a Capitol security officer enters the office asking if we'd be willing to relocate the event outside due to the overwhelming turnout. At this point the request wasn't logistically possible due to the radio setup, but I now knew this would be an interesting rally. You could definitely feel the energy in the room and in the building. The rally itself was pretty intense as there wasn't much room to maneuver. I ended up leaning against a wall about ten or fifteen feet behind the podium while surrounded by people and figurines dotting the hallways.

The magnitude of it all was way more than I expected. People lined up all around and above the main floor chanting for her to run for governor. A chord had certainly been struck. Though it [the rally] ran a bit longer than expected, the people seemed unfazed. All the while I was glad I was able to be there taking it all in while standing in the background, watching a mix of young and old show her their support. Hopefully the future won't hold more of such events. Hopefully they'll be unnecessary.

Even today whenever I go to the mall, grocery store, out to eat, or even to a movie, someone will approach me and ask, "Are you Sally Kern?" I answer yes, but the thought *always* goes through my mind, "Are they for me or against me?" So far, all of them have been for me, thanking me for my stand for traditional marriage.

During the days of the Jesus movement, Kurt Kaiser wrote a song called "Pass It On." It says a spark is all that's needed to get a fire going. If the "Freedom of Speech Rally for Sally" can be a tiny spark used by God to get a fire going in His church, I'll give Him all the glory. If that fire results in a burning desire to stand up for the truth of God's Word, then everything that has come because the Gay and Lesbian Victory Fund posted two minutes and fifty-nine seconds of a little old grandma's speech on YouTube will be worth it all.

PRIVATE ENCOURAGEMENT

Although the rally was a tremendous show of support that brought people from all over Oklahoma as well as from Texas and Kansas to the state capitol, there were two other expressions of support that came my way that were more of a private nature. They border on the miraculous.

Jack and Phyllis Poe live just a few blocks from our house. They're two of my constituents. Jack was an Oklahoma pastor who at the time was the chaplain for the Oklahoma City Police Department. He played a major role in the aftermath of the Murrah Building bombing in

1995 that killed 168 people in Oklahoma City when a truck filled with explosives totally destroyed the nine-story building. When terrorists destroyed the twin towers on September 11, 2001, Jack was called to go to New York City to help counsel the rescue workers. He and Phyllis are godly people who serve the Lord in a very unique way.

Sunday morning, March 9, 2008, just two days after angry homosexuals began bombarding me with thousands of hate e-mails, Jack and Phyllis showed up in our morning worship service. As I entered the auditorium with the choir and looked out over the congregation, I immediately noticed them sitting in the pews. I was not only emotionally drained but also extremely stressed out over the events of the past two days. Just the night before Steve and I had counted the cost of what my public comments might extract from us. You have to realize that although none of us know what the future holds for us, our future was definitely facing some perilous uncertainty.

Upon seeing Jack and Phyllis sitting there, I almost broke into tears because I just knew they had come to offer their support and encouragement. We have a time during our service where Steve shares some prayer concerns and invites people to come forward and pray. This particular morning he asked the church to keep the two of us in their prayers because of what was taking place. Everybody knew their pastor's wife had gotten herself into some hot water, to say the least.

As people began coming forward, so did Jack and Phyllis. But they walked right up onto the platform and motioned for me to come to them. Of course I did. As I approached them, they wrapped me in their arms and began to pray mightily. I began to cry instantly. They cried with me. It was a prayer for protection, wisdom, and strength. As the tears flowed down my face, the stress just seemed to flow right with them. My heart rejoiced in the goodness of God for bringing Jack and Phyllis to our church that day.

But, like newscaster Paul Harvey used to say, "Now for the rest of the story." Jack had been out of town for the past couple of days at a conference. Phyllis had been at home reading and never once turned on the TV or radio and so hadn't heard any news. Jack got home on Saturday night, and before going to bed, Phyllis asked him where they were going to go to church tomorrow. In Jack's capacity as police chaplain, they often visited different churches. He told her he didn't know just yet, to let him sleep on it. Phyllis gets up very early each morning for her prayer time. While praying on Sunday morning, she felt impressed that they should go to Olivet. Jack awakened later and walked in, announcing to her that for some reason he thought they should visit Olivet. So they showed up at our church not knowing one thing about the hell storm that was brewing in the Kerns' lives.

Two people whom God uses on a regular basis to counsel others were divinely sent to counsel and comfort Steve and me that day. Without a doubt I knew that God was in control and would walk me through this experience, ultimately for His glory, for my good, and for the benefit of others. It is moments like this that cause us to sit in awe at the majesty of God. I probably would never have had such a precious revelation of God's divine intervention if I had not been attacked. The truth of Romans 8:28 was revealed to me anew that day. Truly, "all things work together for the good of those who love God: those who are called according to His purpose."

If you're over the hill, as they say, you just might remember the next person God sent to offer me guidance and encouragement through this battle. This woman could certainly say, "Been there, done that." She knew better than anyone else what I was facing, and would continue to face, and her wisdom had been forged in the fires of trial and persecution. Remember the old E. F. Hutton investment ads? It went something like this: "When E. F. Hutton speaks, people listen."

Well, when Anita Bryant spoke, I listened.

Just in case you don't know who Anita Bryant is, let me tell you a little bit about this woman. At age twelve, she had her own TV show. She won the Arthur Godfrey talent competition at age sixteen. At eighteen years of age she was Miss Oklahoma. She was second runner-up in the 1958 Miss America pageant. During her twenties she toured with Bob Hope entertaining American soldiers. For her bravery in going to the front lines, she received the USO's Silver Medallion Award by the National Guard and the Veterans of Foreign Wars Leadership Gold Medallion, along with the Al Jolson Gold Medal Award and Citation.

For twelve years she was the spokeswoman for the Florida Citrus Commission. Name brands such as Coca Cola, Tupperware, Kraft Foods, and Holiday Inns paid Anita to endorse their products. These endorsement contracts were very lucrative. She was the halftime entertainment for Super Bowl V in 1971. Before his death, President Lyndon B. Johnson said he wanted Anita Bryant to sing "The Battle Hymn of the Republic" at his funeral, and she did. During the 1960s and 1970s, she was one of the most successful singers in the world, topping the charts not only in the United States but also in Britain. She had three gold records and recorded forty-five albums. A Gallup poll listed her among the top ten women in the world, and for three consecutive years *Good Housekeeping* magazine named her "the most admired woman in America."[5]

It looked like Anita Bryant had it all. She also had a strong faith in God. When she was eight years old, she gave her life to Jesus Christ and never looked back. Even with all the fame and acclaim she never forgot that it was God who gave it all to her.

But her life changed drastically in 1977. She was living in South Florida with her husband, Bob Green, when Dade County (now Miami-Dade County) passed an ordinance granting anti-discrimination rights to homosexuals. Being widely known not only for her musical talents but also for her vibrant faith, Anita was asked to lead in an effort to get this policy changed. As one who always wanted to honor

God and His Word, she agreed to get involved. The ordinance was successfully repealed largely because of her efforts. She also led a campaign that resulted in the Florida legislature prohibiting homosexuals from adopting children.[6]

Because Anita refused to back down, radical homosexual activists viciously attacked her. They organized boycotts against her corporate sponsors, aroused activist homosexuals all across America to hold protest rallies, enlisted entertainers to blacklist her, and went as far as hitting her in the face with a pie on one very public occasion. She and her family received death threats, kidnapping threats toward her children, bomb scares, hate mail, and even voodoo dolls.[7] In her book *The Anita Bryant Story*, she wrote, "But I've learned to obey God regardless of the consequences."[8] For Anita the consequences were the destruction of her career. The hardships she and her family endured created such pressure that even her marriage crumbled under the weight.

I remember watching news accounts about all this back in 1977. At the time I could hardly believe what I was viewing on TV. Steve was just entering seminary to prepare for the ministry, and our hearts went out to this lady who took such a stand for her faith. We prayed for her and asked God to give us the faith and boldness to do likewise someday if necessary. Her bravery encouraged us back then. Little did I know that one day this bold woman would be personally encouraging me as I was thrust into the same battle she confronted so many years earlier.

It was Tuesday, March 11, 2008, five days after this ordeal over my speech had begun. It was just before noon, and I was sitting in my seat on the House floor when I received a call on my cell phone. I took the call, thinking it might be Steve. A man was on the other end of the line, but it wasn't Steve. He said he was Charlie Dry, Anita Bryant's husband, and told me she wanted to talk with me if I would like to speak with her.

If I would like to talk with her? I couldn't believe she wanted to talk with *me*. Of course, I told him yes, I'd love to speak with her. In less than ten minutes Anita Bryant and I were having a heart-to-heart talk. That conversation meant so much to me because she gave me some of the best advice on how to deal with this situation. And it was coming from someone who knew from experience what I was going through. Her advice was not just theory but heartfelt, practical admonitions that came from a life that had suffered the consequences of the wrath of the radical homosexual movement.

The first thing she encouraged me to do was go to the Scriptures and look up all the verses on fear, being afraid, and trusting the Lord for protection. She told me to memorize them and claim them daily. She knew that the intimidation by homosexuals was intended to create fear in one's heart.

Next she told me to gather my family around me, especially my husband, and honestly discuss what was happening, and then to pray—a lot. She said Satan would attempt to use this situation to create division within my family, especially between my husband and me, and that we had to stand together against this. During this time we needed not only the Lord's strength but also the strength of one another.

She also shared that we needed the strength of the body of Christ and counseled me to seek out consecrated prayer warriors who would stand with my family and me through this. She reminded me that God's Word is truth and stressed that Satan is the enemy seeking to destroy my life, not those who were ridiculing me. Finally, she gave me her number and said I could call her anytime, night or day.

The day the "Rally for Sally" was held at the state capitol, Anita Bryant was not physically present, but she was there in spirit. We had talked about whether or not she should come. After much prayer, Anita felt it would be more beneficial for her to stay at home and pray for me. This woman who'd had the spotlight shine on her thousands of times and was comfortable being in it believed God wanted to establish me in this battle.

As I pondered over what Anita had shared, I was reminded of 2 Corinthians 1:3–4: "Blessed be the God and Father of our Lord Jesus Christ, the Father of mercies and the God of all comfort. He comforts us in all our affliction, so that we may be able to comfort those who are in any kind of affliction, through the comfort we ourselves receive from God."

Rep. Sally Kern, Oklahoma House of Representatives, District 84

I love participating in the Bethany Freedom Parade every Fourth of July. Seeing Oklahomans from all walks of life display their patriotism always makes me wish the American people took more time to show their love for this great country.

David H. Glover/Flying Humans

I was caught completely off-guard in March 2008 when comments I made led to a barrage of hateful e-mail. Since then everything I have done has sparked fresh attacks. This photo was taken when I presented my Oklahoma Citizens' Proclamation for Morality in July 2009. As you can see, the document generated a lot of media attention—and more controversy—but I believe it was a step toward bringing an awakening in our state and, perhaps, in the nation.

This photo was taken with State Rep. Charles Key, Pastor Tom Vineyard of Windsor Hills Baptist Church, and State Rep. Mike Ritze (shown from left, respectively) the week I sponsored Pastor Vineyard as our chaplain of the week. I have a soft spot for this position. Serving as chaplain of the week beginning in 1997 is what motivated my husband, Dr. Steve Kern, to encourage me to run for office.

This is my fourth term in the state House of Representatives, and I still get nervous when debating legislation. Having a seatmate and mentor such as Rep. Sue Tibbs of Tulsa, Oklahoma, who has served six terms in the House, has been a godsend. She is one tough lady with a heart of gold.

Pastor Paul Blair of Fairview Baptist Church has been a great support since I became the target of media attacks. As director of Reclaiming America for Christ, he is taking his own stand for the Christian values that have made this nation strong.

The attacks from the homosexual community allowed me to get to
know Anita Bryant, who faced a similar firestorm in 1977 when she
opposed a gay rights ordinance in Miami. She and worship leader
Dennis Jernigan, who by God's grace no longer lives a gay lifestyle and
is married with nine children, have become great friends to me. They
took this picture with me during the inauguration ceremonies in 2011.

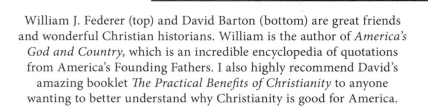

William J. Federer (top) and David Barton (bottom) are great friends and wonderful Christian historians. William is the author of *America's God and Country,* which is an incredible encyclopedia of quotations from America's Founding Fathers. I also highly recommend David's amazing booklet *The Practical Benefits of Christianity* to anyone wanting to better understand why Christianity is good for America.

Sgt. Cindy Crenshaw-Martin is one of the brave soldiers I honored as a veteran of the week. Cindy lost both of her lower extremities in a terrorist bombing in Germany while serving in the Air Force, but I've never heard her complain about losing her legs. She told me she only regrets that she was not able to serve her country longer.

I consider Oklahoma Gov. Mary Fallin a friend and was honored to attend a prayer service for her in January 2011. More than two thousand people joined in prayer for our state's first female governor, which for me was one of the highlights of the gubernatorial inauguration events.

My husband, Steve, came up with the KERNservative campaign slogan.
It's catchy, and it fits me so well. Graduating from Liberal High School
in Liberal, Kansas, is the closest I've ever come to being liberal.

I seem to attract just as much controversy when I present legislation as I do when I give speeches. I received the Mouth of the House award in 2006 for introducing a bill that would have required schools to teach the pros and cons of evolution. Even after debating the bill for more than two hours, my opponents continued to insist that it was just an attempt to teach creationism in public schools. That was not the case, but sadly the measure was not enacted.

This photo was taken with Kansas Gov. Sam Brownback back in 2007 when he was running for president of the United States. I admire his godly witness in politics, which is much needed these days.

I met former Florida Gov. Jeb Bush when he visited Oklahoma in 2010 to promote his Excellence in Education Foundation. At the time of this visit, our state was planning to introduce education reforms modeled after those he implemented in Florida.

My son Jesse and I had a ball at the 2008 Republican National Convention in Minnesota. He became a target amid all the controversy, which as a mother was harder for me to endure than the volumes of hateful e-mail directed toward me.

This picture of several members of the Oklahoma House of Representatives was taken the year we won the annual softball game between the House and Senate. I've always been a huge sports fan. I played shortstop, left field, and pitcher in my younger days, and back then I was the leading base stealer.

I was honored to stand with members of the 2011 Oklahoma
Congressional delegation (from left: Rep. Frank Lucas; Rep. James
Lankford; me and my husband, Steve; Rep. John Sullivan; and Rep.
Tom Cole). I am humbled that God allowed me to be elected to public
office, and I hold everything He gives me with an open hand. No
matter how many hits I take, I care most about His opinion of me. My
prayer is that He finds me faithful to the calling He's given me.

Chapter Six

CAUTION! DANGER AHEAD!

I N THE EARLY MORNING HOURS OF MAY 26, 2002, A FREIGHT
barge on the Arkansas River hit a pylon supporting a long section of bridge along Interstate 40 near Webbers Falls, Oklahoma. As
a result of the impact, a five-hundred-foot section of the bridge crumbled and fell into the rain-swollen river below. Eleven vehicles fell into
the fast-moving waters. Fourteen people lost their lives.[1]

You may have heard reports of this tragedy on the news. What
you may not have heard is why the death toll wasn't even higher.

Two fishermen in their boat heard the noise of the impact and
saw the bridge give way. They watched in disbelief as several cars—
traveling along the highway at full speed—plunged over the edge.
Frantic, they scrambled to find a way to stop the traffic. Thinking fast,
one of the fishermen pulled out some emergency flares he carried and
began firing them into the lanes of oncoming traffic. One flare hit
the windshield of a semitruck, and the driver slammed on his brakes,
stopping at the edge of the collapsed bridge. Seeing the danger, the
trucker moved the semi to block the traffic, sparing scores of lives.[2]

I believe most of us would do the same thing if placed in the situation of those fishermen. What kind of human being—not to mention

what kind of Christian—would simply go on about his or her business after seeing unsuspecting people hurtling toward disaster? I know I couldn't. As others have said after going to Africa and witnessing the famine and suffering there, "I have seen. Therefore I am responsible."

After a decade in inner-city ministry, *I have seen.* I have seen the emotional, psychological, and spiritual pain the practice of the homosexual lifestyle produces. And after attending that conference I mentioned at the outset of this book, I became responsible for what I learned there about the stealthy political agenda that had already successfully removed good men and women from office.

You see, at the root of the controversy surrounding me and the comments I made in that speech are two separate and distinct issues. One issue is the well-financed, stealthy strategy to change America's view of homosexuality. I'll talk more about that in this chapter. The second issue is a more fundamental one that I'll discuss through the remainder of this book. Do Bible-believing Christians in today's politically correct America still have the freedom to repeat what the Bible says about truth and morality? Or has openly professing something that is clearly stated in Scripture become a disqualification for holding public office or even being heard in the public square?

In other words: Are we allowed to warn others of danger ahead? Must we remain silent when we know there is a bridge out ahead?

The signs are obvious that there is great danger ahead for America if our society continues down the road toward tolerance and moral acceptance of homosexuality. Many people far more intelligent and learned than I am have already written about and loudly proclaimed the disastrous consequences America will face if we continue down this path. For this reason I will not seek to reinvent the wheel but will briefly mention some of the dangers. If you want more detail, you will find a list of excellent resources to choose from at the back of this book. They will open your eyes to the very present and real dangers that are confronting us.

Of course, as in any age of danger, there are many people who don't want to know the truth. They are either willingly deceived or self-deceived. For example, thousands of e-mails were sent to me saying there is no homosexual agenda. Yet the proof of a homosexual agenda can be easily found if one takes the time to look for it. In 1987 an article published in the gay magazine *Guide,* titled "The Overhauling of Straight America," outlined a homosexual agenda that was already being advanced. It was written by two Harvard professors, Marshall Kirk and Erastus Pill, a pseudonym for Hunter Madsen. The opening paragraph in the article states:

> The first order of business is desensitization of the American public concerning gays and gay rights. To desensitize the public is to help it view homosexuality with indifference instead of with keen emotion. Ideally, we would have straights register differences in sexual preference the way they register different tastes for ice cream or sports games: she likes strawberry and I like vanilla; he follows baseball and I follow football. No big deal.[3]

Without a doubt, this order of business is well on its way to being accomplished. Just turn on the TV, and you'll find shows filled with homosexual characters on almost every channel, even in cartoons.

Hollywood has never been much of a friend to those who are fighting to preserve marriages and families in our nation. On the contrary, since the sixties many elites in the multibillion-dollar entertainment industry have done their best to undermine our society's traditional view of marriage. In movies, television programs, and songs we consistently see wrong held up as right and right denounced as intolerance. And, more than ever, we're seeing efforts to redefine the terms *marriage* and *family* into meaninglessness.

In this battle Hollywood is doing its part to try to "normalize" homosexual marriage, gay adoption, and "alternative" forms of family composition. *Will & Grace* and *Brokeback Mountain* are recent examples. But a new crop of movies and television series represent an escalation in the war on marriage. One of the boldest of these is the HBO series *Big Love*, which followed the trials of a polygamist man with three wives.

THE TIP OF THE SPEAR

Conservative social observers such as Stanley Kurtz of the Hoover Institution have been warning us for some time that the push for gay marriage was just the tip of the spear. He has predicted that the same arguments currently being used to advocate for homosexual marriage will quickly be followed by moves to legitimize polygamy and polyamory ("marriage" among multiple individuals).

Writing about such efforts already under way in Canada, Kurtz stated:

> The way to abolish marriage, without seeming to abolish it, is to redefine the institution out of existence. If everything can be marriage, pretty soon nothing will be marriage. Legalize gay marriage, followed by multi-partner marriage, and pretty soon the whole idea of marriage will be meaningless. At that point, Canada can move to what [Martha] Bailey [a Queens University law professor who advocated for the decriminalization of polygamy] and her friends really want: an infinitely flexible relationship system that validates any conceivable family

arrangement, regardless of the number or gender of partners.[4]

In a similar way the media mainstreaming of homosexuality is everywhere. "The Overhauling of Straight America" goes on to detail six strategies that, if followed, will transform America into a nation that fully accepts homosexuality. These six strategies are:

1. *Talk about gays and gayness as loudly and as often as possible.* "The principle behind this advice is simple: almost any behavior begins to look normal if you are exposed to enough of it at close quarters and among your acquaintances."[5]

2. *Portray gays as victims, not as aggressive challengers.* "In any campaign to win over the public, gays must be cast as victims in need of protection so that straights will be inclined by reflex to assume the role of protector."[6]

3. *Give protectors a just cause.* "A media campaign that casts gays as society's victims and encourages straights to be their protectors must make it easier for those to respond to assert and explain their new protectiveness."[7]

4. *Make gays look good.* "In order to make a Gay Victim sympathetic to straights you have to portray him as Everyman.... The campaign should paint gays as superior pillars of society."[8]

5. *Make the victimizers look bad.* "At a later stage of the media campaign for gay rights—long after other gay ads have become commonplace—it will be time to get tough

with remaining opponents. To be blunt, they must be vilified."[9]

6. *Solicit funds: the buck stops here.* "Any massive campaign of this kind would require unprecedented expenditures for months or even years—an unprecedented fundraising drive."[10]

Need more proof that this agenda is real and on the move? "The Overhauling of Straight America" was so well received by the homosexual community, Kirk and Madsen followed it up with *After the Ball: How America Will Conquer Its Fear and Hatred of Gays in the '90s.* This book, written in 1989, recommends using propaganda techniques, psychology, and the media to dupe the American public. For example, in the book the authors write:

> The campaign we outline in this book, though complex, depends centrally upon a program of unabashed propaganda, firmly grounded in long established principles of psychology and advertising.[11]

In other words, these two men advocate using sophisticated techniques to brainwash society into believing that the homosexual lifestyle is just another alternative way of life. In the book, the authors tell homosexual activists to promote the idea that they are born that way when they write, "We argue that, for all practical purposes, gays should be considered to have been born gay."[12] There is overwhelming evidence that this is precisely the playbook that has been followed in the twenty years since the book's publication. It would seem the American people have been purposely manipulated into accepting the homosexual lifestyle.

In the face of such facts, we're still assured by many that there is no such thing as a homosexual agenda, that it's all in the fevered minds of religious zealots and "homophobes." The clear truth is, there is a long-term strategy to produce a generation of Americans who view sexual preference as no more significant a matter than a preference for rocky road ice cream.

As you might expect, schools have become a key target in this indoctrination process. On May 19, 2009, Kevin Jennings was appointed Deputy Assistant Secretary of the Department of Education, Office of Safe and Drug-Free Schools. Who is Kevin Jennings? He is the founder of the Gay, Lesbian, and Straight Education Network (GLSEN), whose official mission is to make schools "safe" for homosexual students. That includes encouraging teachers to incorporate homosexual-themed material into the curriculum.[13]

While Jennings was leading GLSEN, the organization sought to teach pro-homosexual themes to children as young as kindergarteners because, as a GLSEN representative claimed in a 1997 seminar, children at that age are "developing their superego" and "that's when the saturation process needs to begin."[14]

Please forgive the graphic explanation, but during a 2000 conference hosted by GLSEN and open to children as young as twelve years old, panelists participated in a very graphic discussion of "fisting," the act of forcing one's entire hand into another person's rectum or vagina. Rather than decry the activity, the panelists said that "it gets a bad rap," and that it was about "intimacy" and "exploration."[15] At the same conference involving the "fisting" controversy, teenage girls were required to role-play as two infatuated lesbians, and children were told that they could make an "informed decision" not to use a condom during premarital sexual activity.[16]

Jennings wrote the foreword to the book *Queering Elementary Education*, endorsing a work that sought to reaffirm "sissy boys," hoped to reeducate parents opposed to teaching homosexual culture in grade schools, and claimed that "presumed heterosexuality...is an artifact of oppression."[17] And although Jennings's office leads the Department of Education's initiatives regarding the prevention of drug abuse and drug-induced violence, Jennings admitted in his memoir that he was a habitual marijuana user during his high school years.[18]

A Generation in Crisis

If youth come to view homosexuality as an alternative lifestyle without dangerous consequences, we can expect to see an increase in HIV and AIDS. In fact, we already are. According to the Centers for Disease Control and Prevention (CDC), the numbers of young homosexual men diagnosed with the HIV infection is rising at a heartbreaking 12 percent each year. This increase is ten times higher than in the homosexual community overall.[19] CDC statistics also show that young people under the age of twenty-five make up almost half of all new sexually transmitted disease infections in the United States.[20]

My husband and I have seen up close the suffering and heartache sexually transmitted diseases create. Under my husband's leadership, Olivet Baptist recently launched an outreach to people with HIV/AIDS. Our new center in the inner city offers free, confidential testing as well as pretest and posttest counseling.

As I mentioned earlier, one of the greatest obstacles to advancing this agenda is the Bible's teaching that homosexuality is a sin and not God's design for His children. In order for the radical homosexuals to remove all obstacles for total acceptance of their lifestyle, they must do away with traditional Christian teachings on sex. Sadly, many liberal pastors are furthering this agenda by twisting the meaning of Scripture in ways that remove its clear condemnations and prohibitions of homosexuality.

The mainstream media are doing their part in this effort. You may remember, for example, the 2008 *Newsweek* cover story that claimed that the Bible supports homosexuality and gay marriage.[21]

At the same time, you can expect to see an attempt to silence criticism of these efforts through hate crimes laws. As is already the case in Canada, such laws will severely limit our First Amendment right of free speech and freedom of worship.

Of course, all of this puts us on a slippery slope. No doubt you've seen the letters GLBT. Sometimes they're listed LGBT. Other times LGBTQ. These letters stand for gay, lesbian, bisexual, and transgender. The Q is for queer (or as some say, "questioning"). This acronym cluster seems to get a little longer every year. New sexual orientations and gender identities are emerging all the time. Recent additions include pansexuality and polysexuality.

Before our eyes the unspeakable is being legitimized and mainstreamed. And as this twisted alphabet soup pours out of the dark corners of our culture and into the streets, don't be surprised to see San Francisco's "Folsom Street Fair" duplicated in cities around our country. "And what is the Folsom Street Fair?" you ask. You'll be sorry you did.

This spectacle regularly draws upwards of four hundred thousand participants and gawkers, largely from the leather and BDSM (bondage, dominance, and submission; sadism and masochism) subculture, who are encouraged to participate in sadomasochistic activities.[22] This has become the third largest public event in California, right behind the Tournament of Roses Parade.[23] Unbelievably, some parents bring their children to this event where sex acts and perverse rituals are performed in broad daylight.

This won't be the worst of it, unfortunately. Louis P. Sheldon, in his book *The Agenda: The Homosexual Plan to Change America*, says the radical homosexual activist's "goal is to enforce acceptance and legitimization of their lifestyle and to overpower and overwhelm by sheer force anyone who dares to stand in their way."[24] Think this can't happen in America where we have the First Amendment, freedom of speech, and freedom of religion? Consider this. Lesbian lawyer Barbara Findlay in an address to fellow homosexual/lesbian rights activists said, "The legal struggle for queer rights will one day be a showdown between freedom of religion versus sexual orientation."[25]

Do you grasp the significance of that statement? The radical homosexual activists do. They understand the true nature of this battle. Christians don't. They don't want to offend anyone. After all, the Bible says, "Do not judge, so that you won't be judged" (Matt. 7:1). It's time people realize that this verse has become a so-called biblical way of restating the secular slogan "live and let live." No sincere Christian would dare live by the standard of "live and let live." Surely they know about James 5:20, which states, "... whoever turns a sinner from the error of his way will save his life from death and cover a multitude of sins."

Need more proof there is a battle for the mind and soul of our nation going on? Paula Ettelbrick, former legal director of the Lambda Legal Defense and Education Fund and current director of the International Gay and Lesbian Human Rights Commission, said, "Being queer is more than setting up house, sleeping with a person of the same gender, and seeking state approval for doing so.... Being queer means pushing the parameters of sex, sexuality, and family, and in the process, transforming the very fabric of society.... We must keep our eyes on the goal... of radically reordering society's view of family."[26]

Steve Warren, a spokesman for the controversial homosexual group ACT UP, wrote in a similar vein in an article titled "Warning to the Homophobes" in a 1987 issue of *The Advocate*. In it he promised that "we are going to force you [Christians] to recant everything you have believed or said about sexuality.... We will in all likelihood want to expunge a number of passages from your Scriptures and rewrite others eliminating preferential treatment of marriage and using words that will allow for homosexual interpretations of passages."[27]

Compassion and Truth

Meanwhile, Christians consistently are called hate mongers and bigots simply because they stand by the Bible's boundaries for healthy sexual activity—boundaries that are constantly being validated by medical, sociological, and empirical data. Homosexual activists reinforce this charge of hate mongering and bigotry by asking why the God of the Bible would disapprove of them when they were "born that way."

Countless university studies and research initiatives have attempted to find some identifiable physical marker that would justify such claims. A few have initially claimed to find a "gay gene" or some other physiological cause for homosexuality, but upon close scrutiny, no genetic cause for homosexuality has been conclusively demonstrated.[28]

Most respected researchers attribute homosexuality to a combination of social, biological, and psychological factors. Gay men frequently report having had an absent or abusive father, a domineering mother, and/or having been molested at an early age.[29] Likewise, some studies have shown that homosexual women are almost twice as likely as heterosexual women to report having been the victims of some sort of sexual abuse early in life.[30] My heart goes out to people who have experienced such pain and victimization—even more so now that they are being victimized by a deception that they were always meant to be that way.

As Robert H. Knight, one of the individuals who drafted the federal Defense of Marriage Act, writes, "Americans for too long have been pummeled with the idea that people are 'born gay.' The people who most need to hear the truth are those who mistakenly believe they have no chance themselves for change. It is both more compassionate and truthful to give them hope than to serve them up politically motivated, unproven creations like the 'gay gene.'"[31] Unfortunately, many in the church have believed this lie too and so feel no need to share hope or help with these individuals.

Perhaps you recall the sixties-era TV series called *Lost in Space*. It was a sci-fi adventure about the Robinson family, the villain Smith, and a robot. Will Robinson and the robot were friends. Often the robot would warn Will of danger by yelling, "Danger, Will Robinson! Danger!"

Today there are many voices crying out, "Danger, America! Danger!" They are also shouting, "Wake up, church! Wake up!" But warnings are only good if they are heeded, and in time.

Many years ago Abraham Lincoln made a statement that prophetically depicts what is happening to America today. He said:

> At what point then is the approach of danger to be expected? I answer, if it ever reach us, it must spring up amongst us. It cannot come from abroad. If destruction be our lot, we must ourselves be its author and finisher. As a nation of freemen, we must live through all time, or die by suicide.[32]

One of the snippets from my now infamous speech that has been replayed endlessly by my critics on the Left is the sentence in which I say that the homosexual lifestyle and its agenda are "a greater threat than terrorism." If I hadn't been in such a hurry to hit all my points, I would have elaborated on that thought in a way that wouldn't have left me so open to outrage and demagoguery. Nevertheless, Lincoln's quote goes to the heart of what I was trying to communicate.

Terrorists seek to do damage to our nation and to its people. Yet we, the American people, are bringing the wholesale destruction of our nation upon ourselves as we wholeheartedly embrace homosexuality, a lifestyle proven to be dangerous and deadly. We are currently very vigilant against the terrorist threats against us. We seem oblivious to this more pervasive inner decay.

My hope and prayer is that this book and the hate-storm I've been through will in some way help to change that dangerous complacency.

Chapter Seven

MORALITY, TRUTH, AND TOLERANCE

"I T'S TIME TO WISE UP AND RISE UP." IT'S A PHRASE I'VE
repeated many times as I've been invited to speak to various civic
and Christian groups in the months since I was suddenly shoved into
the front lines of the culture war. It is something I believe strongly.
In the previous chapter I spoke of a dangerous complacency among
the good people of America's vast, silent majority. I am convinced we
need another "great awakening" among our nation's people of faith.

On July 2, 2009, I participated in a special event that was a small
but significant step toward bringing about such an awakening. There,
in the rotunda of the state capitol, I was joined by more than two hundred other Oklahomans as well as like-minded citizens from around
the country for a public reading of a bold proclamation. It was widely
reported that I wrote this proclamation. But it is more accurate to say
that I, along with some wonderful historians and Christian scholars,
assembled it. We took key quotes from our nation's Founding Fathers,
such as John Adams, James Madison, and Thomas Jefferson; a portion of the preamble of the Oklahoma constitution; along with relevant, time-tested wisdom from the Bible and wove them together into

a powerful declaration of truth. It is a declaration that points our way out of the dark swamp of moral and cultural decay into which we have sunk as a people.

Crafting proclamations such as these is not a new innovation or fad. They are a time-honored tradition in this nation. For example, on March 16, 1776, the Continental Congress, at what those men called a time of "impending calamity and distress; when the Liberties of America are imminently endangered," issued a proclamation "publickly [sic] to acknowledge the over ruling providence of God."[1] They also called for a day of "Public Worship." President Lincoln's "Thanksgiving Proclamation" of 1863 is one of the great documents of American history as well as one of our most beautiful expressions of civic faith.

Countless proclamations have been drawn throughout America's history, and it was in that tradition that we penned ours. Here are the words of that document in its entirety.[2]

OKLAHOMA CITIZENS' PROCLAMATION FOR MORALITY

We the People of Oklahoma, Invoking the guidance of Almighty God, in order to secure and perpetuate the blessing of Liberty; to secure just and rightful Government; to promote our mutual Welfare and Happiness, do establish this proclamation and call upon the people of the great State of Oklahoma, and our fellow Patriots in these United States of America who look to the Lord for guidance, to acknowledge the need for a national awakening of righteousness in our land.

WHEREAS, "It is Religion and Morality alone, which can establish the Principles upon which Freedom can securely stand" (John Adams);[3] and

WHEREAS, "We have no government armed with power capable of contending with human passions unbridled by Religion and Morality" (John Adams);[4] and

WHEREAS, "Our Constitution was made only for a Moral and Religious people" (John Adams);[5] and

WHEREAS, "We have staked the whole future of American civilization, not upon the power of government…but upon the capacity of mankind for self-government, upon the capacity of each and all of us to govern ourselves, to control ourselves, to sustain ourselves according to the Ten Commandments of God" (James Madison);[6] and

WHEREAS, "Freedom is not a gift bestowed upon us by other men, but a right that belongs to us by the laws of God" (Benjamin Franklin);[7] and

WHEREAS, "God who gave us life gave us liberty"[8] and "can the liberties of a nation be thought secure when we have removed their only firm basis, a conviction in the minds of the people that these liberties are of the Gift of God" (Thomas Jefferson);[9] and

WHEREAS, "Whether any free government can be permanent, where the public worship of God, and the support of Religion, constitute no part of the policy or duty of the state" (Joseph Story);[10] and

WHEREAS, "We hold sacred the rights of conscience, and promise to the people…the free and undisturbed exercise of their religion" (Roger Sherman);[11] and

WHEREAS, "This great nation was founded, not by religionists, but by Christians" (Patrick Henry);[12] and

WHEREAS, "When you…exercise the right of voting for public officers, let it be impressed upon your mind that God commands you to choose just men who will rule in the fear of God" (Noah Webster);[13] and

WHEREAS, "The principles of genuine Liberty and of wise laws and administrations are to be drawn from the Bible" (Noah Webster);[14] and

WHEREAS, the people of Oklahoma have a strong tradition of reliance upon the Creator of the Universe; and

WHEREAS, we believe our economic woes are consequences of our greater national moral crisis; and

WHEREAS, this nation has become a world leader in promoting abortion, pornography, same-sex marriage, sex trafficking, divorce, illegitimate births, child abuse, and many other forms of debauchery; and

WHEREAS, alarmed that the Government of the United States of America is forsaking the rich Christian heritage upon which this nation was built; and

WHEREAS, grieved that the Office of the President of these United States has refused to uphold the long-held tradition of past presidents in giving recognition to our National Day of Prayer; and

WHEREAS, deeply disturbed that the Office of the President of these United States disregards the biblical admonitions to live clean and pure lives by proclaiming an entire month to an immoral behavior;

NOW THEREFORE, BE IT RESOLVED that we the undersigned elected officials of the people of Oklahoma, religious leaders and citizens of the State of Oklahoma, appealing to the Supreme Judge of the world, solemnly declare that the HOPE of the great State of Oklahoma and of these United States, rests upon the Principles of Religion and Morality as put forth in the HOLY BIBLE; and

BE IT RESOLVED that we, the undersigned, believers in the One True God and His only Son, call upon all to join with us in recognizing that "Blessed is the Nation whose God is the Lord,"[15] and humbly implore all who love Truth and Virtue to live above reproach in the sight of God and man with a firm reliance on the leadership and protection of Almighty God; and

BE IT RESOLVED that we, the undersigned, humbly call upon Holy God, our Creator, Sustainer, and Redeemer, to have mercy on this nation, to stay His hand of judgment, and grant a national awakening of righteousness and Christian renewal as we repent of our great sin.

Signed on the second day of July in the year of our Lord Christ Two Thousand and Nine.

The signing event we held in the state capitol was a moving experience, even though a small but noisy cluster of protesters joined the group of a few hundred of us there to mark the launch of a drive to gather signatories from around the state. To their credit, the protesters were largely quiet while I read the proclamation. But shortly thereafter they broke into chants of "Shame on you! Shame on you!"

I will never be pressured and harangued, however, into ceasing to remind a culture that has lost its way of the principles upon which it was founded. Nor will I ever be persuaded to feel shame for proclaiming the message that there is life and freedom in the eternal principles of the Bible.

In a similar way to what they had done with my comments in the speech that had been secretly recorded, my critics on the Left and a sympathetic media seized on a single phrase from the lengthy proclamation and used a caricature of it to put a negative spin on the entire noble effort. They uniformly focused on the clause that said: "WHEREAS, we believe our economic woes are consequences of our greater national moral crisis." The common headline then became "Rep. Sally Kern Holds 'Morality Rally,' Blames Gays for Economic Woes."

Of course, as you just read for yourself, that is a gross distortion of the message of the document. As I pointed out in my comments at the event and in the press conference afterward, if this document represents an indictment of anyone, it is an indictment of the church for failing in her commission to be what Jesus called "salt and light" in Matthew 5:13–16.

Amid all the criticism and unfair media spin, I also received some wonderful words of encouragement. They were like water in the desert for Steve and me. One very meaningful note of endorsement came from David Barton, the founder of the indispensable WallBuilders organization, which provides educational resources about America's Christian foundation. David sent an e-mail out to his extensive list of subscribers that said, in part:

The national news all too often highlights political leaders who do not represent the values of people of faith; consequently, many God-fearing citizens wrongly believe that few elected officials share our moral and religious convictions. But such a conclusion is wrong. There are literally hundreds of elected officials at the state level (and even scores in Congress) who do not only share but are outspoken about our Judeo-Christian values.

One such official is Rep. Sally Kern of the Oklahoma House of Representatives. Rep. Kern recently introduced a Proclamation on Morality that was signed at the State Capitol by numerous elected officials and religious leaders. We thought you might enjoy reading her proclamation, filled with powerful quotes made by America's Founding Fathers.[16]

Still, the proclamation signing triggered a fresh wave of attack on us. It is not surprising that when people like me make an assertion of something being "truth," it provokes a strong negative reaction from the culture at large. Postmodern, post-Christian America has largely rejected the concept that there are moral absolutes or any such thing as "absolute truth." And I am convinced this is the primary issue in the culture war that is raging between the forces of secular humanism on one side and those who believe the Bible is the standard for truth on the other. This is the very conflict that I've been thrust into because of my stand for traditional values. As with belief in God, you either believe in the existence of absolute truth or you don't.

Unchanging Truth

In his excellent book *Right From Wrong*, Josh McDowell defines absolute truth as "that which is true for all people, for all times, for all places."[17] I like that. It's very simple yet profound, because acceptance of absolute truth is at the very core of biblical Christianity. Jesus prayed, "Sanctify them by the truth; Your word is truth" (John 17:17). Remove the concept of absolute truth, and the power of the Bible is diluted and its authority to speak to the issues of homosexuality, marriage, or any other topic, for that matter, is diminished if not destroyed.

Does truth change over time? If it does, then it isn't *absolute*. According to a January 2000 Barna Research Group poll, some 38 percent of adult Americans—Christians and non-Christians alike—stated they believed in absolute truth.[18] That was a historically low number at the time. Yet, less than two years later, the same pollster found that the already low percentage of people who believe in absolute truth had dropped to 22 percent.[19] Subsequent polls have shown only a modest improvement. In 2009 roughly a third (34 percent) of American adults believed in absolute truth.[20]

One thing seems absolutely certain—as a nation, we lack confidence that some things are true "for all people, for all times, for all places." And this is the case even among Christians. Of course, it follows logically that if there are no absolute truths, then nothing can objectively be declared "right" or "wrong" and, least of all, "evil." And yet for a few weeks in 2001, evil made a brief comeback in the minds and vocabularies of our citizens.

I can recall September 11, 2001, as if it were yesterday. We were giving a standardized test that day that lasted two and a half hours. About midway through the test I opened my classroom door to call for a proctor, and I saw one of my colleagues standing outside in the hall with a look of shock on her face. She was African American, but her face looked white as pure snow as she told me of the horrifying terrorist attack.

If you are like me and most other Americans, you watched the collapse of the World Trade Center towers on your television screen with a mixture of horror, sorrow, and rage. I also suspect there was a word in your mind to describe the actions that brought such grief and death to so many people: evil.

That word was in my mind too, as well as in the minds of every sane person in America. In our "postmodern," everything-is-relative world, evil wasn't supposed to exist anymore. It was supposed to be an artifact of a bygone, old-fashioned era where people actually believed in things like objective truth, right, and wrong. But in those terrifying moments, our culture's perspective changed.

For a season, our nation was jolted out of its complacency by the sheer wickedness of the attacks. Almost immediately our vocabulary—including that of otherwise politically correct journalists, politicians, and law enforcement officials—became downright theological.

The events of September 11 gave us a devastating argument against moral relativism: the existence of evil in the world. If evil exists, then good must exist as well. So, out of the rubble of ground zero, the truth of the absolutes began to reemerge with extraordinary poignancy and power—at least for a little while.

Following the September 11 attacks on our nation, Steven Jukes, the global head of news for Reuters wire service, wrote an internal memo to the company's reporters. In it he said, "We all know that one man's terrorist is another man's freedom fighter and that Reuters upholds the principle that we do not use the word terrorist."[21]

What an amazing example of relativism in action. Contrary to what many in our day try to tell themselves, evil isn't an opinion or a perspective or a frame of reference. It is a force alive and well on Planet Earth. And if we are to know, promote, and experience good, we must begin by acknowledging the reality of evil.

By the time the Bush administration was coming to a close, surveys showed that a full third of Americans suspected that "... federal officials assisted in the 9/11 terrorist attacks or took no action to stop them so the United States could go to war in the Middle East."[22] What heartbreaking evidence that a huge segment of our society has lost the ability to think clearly, in large part because they have abandoned the grounding, orienting power of belief in moral absolutes. They stumble through life with no fixed stars by which to navigate or determine their position.

Contrary to what Oprah or Hollywood or even the National Council of Churches would try to tell us, our beliefs and our actions do matter. Morality matters, and we deny the existence of right and wrong at our peril. The Bible's revelation that the world is fallen and populated by sinners (myself included) armed with the gift of free will gives us the answer to the age-old question of why we see so much suffering and heartache in the world.

The British Christian writer G. K. Chesterton was once asked by the *London Times* to write an essay on the topic "What's wrong with the world?" Chesterton's essay amounted to four words: "Dear Sirs, I am."[23]

John Newton, the man who in the 1700s wrote the hymn "Amazing Grace" after finding Christ and abandoning his involvement in the slave trade, knew that natural inclination toward evil very well. Referring to God, Newton once wrote, "By nature I was too blind to know Him, too proud to trust Him, too obstinate to serve Him, too base-minded to love Him."[24]

Our natural bent toward selfishness and sin is no small matter. It tends to wound everything and everyone it touches—including the person who perpetrates the evil. The fact is, most of the things described as "sin" in the Bible are destructive to self and/or others. Viewed correctly, God's laws are some of the highest evidence of His love. The Ten Commandments are a compassionate call for people to stop hurting themselves and each other.

Uncivil Disagreement

As you have already seen, arguments like the ones I have put forth above are not very popular in today's "enlightened" and "progressive" environment. The cultural elites of our day have a word for the belief that there are some things that are just plain "wrong." They call it *intolerance*.

As I've learned the hard way, to take a stand for moral absolutes in the current cultural climate is to invite the hostility of today's pop culture philosophers. But it is a stand well worth taking because the health and long-term survival of our nation depend on it.

Our world has turned upside down. For the preachers of moral relativism, virtue is now considered a vice. It seems we have fallen into the very trap John Adams wrote about in his diary on February 9, 1772:

> We see every Day, that our Imaginations are so strong and our Reason so weak, the Charms of Wealth and Power are so enchanting, and the Belief of future Punishments so faint, that Men find Ways to persuade themselves, to believe any Absurdity, to submit to any Prostitution, rather than forego their Wishes and Desires. Their Reason becomes at last an eloquent Advocate on the Side of their Passions, and [they] bring themselves to believe that black is white, that Vice is Virtue, that Folly is Wisdom and Eternity a Moment.[25]

Most people today wonder whether there is any such thing as a standard by which we can separate truth from lies or right from wrong. Many question whether we should even try. Useful, meaningful words like *sin*, *wickedness*, and *evil* sound wildly old-fashioned to the modern ear. Using them is an invitation to mockery, ostracism, and soon, perhaps, persecution.

Meanwhile, everyone's greatest fear is apparently an accusation of being judgmental or prudish. This is a particularly powerful weapon being used against Christians. People who take the Bible seriously and strive to live their lives by its precepts are very familiar with Jesus's warning to "Judge not, that ye be not judged" (Matt. 7:1, KJV) and are sensitive to any suggestion that they are violating a biblical principle. This vulnerability in Christians overlays the near-universal human desire to not appear mean, hurtful, or close-minded. The current crop of postmodern libertines have learned this and now reflexively club Christians over the head with it every time one tries to make an argument based on "right and wrong" or absolute truth.

Countless e-mails I have received have contained some version of this tactic. Many cite the "judge not" verse from Matthew or "He that is without sin among you, let him first cast a stone at her" (John 8:7, KJV). It's interesting that those who quote Jesus's words about the "first stone" never go on to cite what He told that woman who had been caught in adultery. He said, "Go, and sin no more" (v. 11, KJV). Jesus clearly believed in the existence of sin, that it was destructive and damning, and that it was appropriate to call it such.

A few of the messages accusing me of being judgmental were at least civil. Most were more along these lines (again, I have deleted the obscenities but left grammar and spelling as I received it):

> You are a dirty [profanity] closeted lesbian [profanity]! How dare you judge others? Do you read the bible? Didn't you ever read the passage about those not judging others...you are far from God. You are the [profanity] devil for spreading lies and HATE! SHAME ON YOU HILLBILLY [profanity]!!

> YOU are the real threat to society! You are a very ignorant and evil woman - a woman who parrots vile platitudes

against a group of people. Your words do not indicate faith but a deep seated animus toward an identity trait. You do not deserve to lead and you do not deserve to speak for Christ.

You apparently are too ignorant to realize that you are neither an American nor a Christian in your views. If you really think that equality and freedom are somehow a nefarious plot by the gay community to "distort" our Constitution, then I am appalled that you were actually allowed to teach children, much less serve in the Oklahoma legislature. You need to re-read the Constitution and the Bible. In particular, you need to re-read Jesus' teaching that you should judge not, lest ye be judged, and that he who is without sin should cast the first stone.

I could cite thousands of others, but I'll spare you. The point is, it appears that few people understand the message of Jesus or that the New Testament calls followers of Christ to be discerning, watchful, bold, vocal, yet loving champions of truth. This book is not the place for a full treatment of these theological issues. Let it suffice to say that any person who thinks being a Christian means not being allowed to speak up in the face of a coordinated propaganda campaign designed to mainstream what the Bible calls abominations doesn't have a very firm grasp of what the Bible teaches.

Clearly, affirming absolute truth no longer seems reasonable to many Americans. In fact, it seems downright small-minded, mean-spirited, and—the ultimate sin in our day—insensitive. (God forbid anyone should ever accuse us of "insensitivity.") Even the gentlest reminder of the relevance of moral standards is viewed as an affront in our "politically correct" society. It may even be considered a "hate crime" now that President Obama has signed new hate crimes legislation into law. This is no exaggeration if Canada is any example.

To get a glimpse of where we may be headed, note that in 2002 a pastor in Alberta wrote a letter to the editor of his local newspaper expressing his opinion that homosexuality was a sin. Upon learning of the letter's publication, a local professor took offense at the pastor's comments. So, did he submit a vigorous rebuttal for publication in the paper? Oh, no. He filed a complaint with Alberta's Human Rights Commission, the government entity empowered to sniff out and punish "hate speech" and general insensitivity to others' feelings. The commission indeed ruled that the pastor's letter "was likely to expose gay persons to more hatred in the community."[26]

Fortunately the decision was overturned upon appeal.[27] The Court of Queen's Bench of Alberta ruled that in order to be considered hate speech, the pastor's letter would have had to incite people to engage in discriminatory practices. Yet the court battle had an intimidating effect, and Christians became afraid to freely proclaim the absolute truth of Scripture.[28]

Intolerant Tolerance

By tossing the concepts of right and wrong in the garbage heap, our culture has come to value all ideas as equally valid. To save our nation, you and I must stand against this seductive trend. To stop our cultural slide down the slope already traveled by the great fallen nations and empires of history, we must make ourselves enemies of evil. Not enemies of *people*, mind you, but enemies of a false and dangerous worldview that denies the very existence of evil. To quote G. K. Chesterton again, "Unless a man becomes the enemy of such an evil, he will not even become its slave, but rather its champion....God Himself will not help us to ignore evil, but only to defy and defeat it."[29]

The pervading moral relativism has brought us to a point in which our society is prepared to tolerate anything and everything with one exception—the person who believes in moral absolutes and says so aloud.

In digging out of the mountains of e-mail abuse under which I've been buried, I've learned a few things. Based on my experience, tolerance really means, "Agree with me or I'll demonize you." It means, "If you say anything disapproving of my lifestyle, you're engaging in hate speech." But if tens of thousands send you e-mail messages filled with threats, profanity, obscenity, and belittling comments about your faith, then that's your own fault. You had it coming.

That was precisely the assertion of Chuck Wolfe, president of the Gay and Lesbian Victory Fund, when he told the *Urban Tulsa Weekly* that any violence threatened against me was my own fault. "If somebody is saying something bad to her, it's because of her words. It's her words that are responsible for the action."[30]

After voters in California approved Proposition 8 in the November 2008 election—amending the state constitution in a way that ensured marriage remained defined as the union of one man and one woman—the retribution and backlash against those who voted for the measure began almost immediately.

For example, the names and addresses of contributors to the pro-Proposition 8 initiative were publicized, with some experiencing harassment and persecution. Some contributors—Scott Eckern,[31] creative director of the California Musical Theater, and Richard Raddon,[32] director of the Los Angeles Film Festival, just to name two—were forced out of their jobs by pressure from homosexual activist groups and boycotts. And because postelection analysis showed that African Americans voted overwhelmingly in favor of Proposition 8, there were several protests that resulted in ugly racial incidents.[33]

This one-sided view of tolerance is not limited to the homosexual political agenda. In 2010, America's largest public school system, the New York City Department of Education, allowed the menorah, a symbol of the Jewish faith, and the star and crescent, a symbol of Islam, to be displayed on school property. But the symbol of the Christian faith, a nativity scene, was expelled and nowhere to be found.[34] A New Hampshire town refused to allow a Christian nonprofit organization to build an electronic sign on private property along a public road because they said its message—Bible verses that change daily—would distract motorists.[35] In Florida, a Christian couple who managed an apartment complex was fired for being "too religious."[36]

This is the twisted logic that will surely characterize the application and enforcement of our freshly broadened federal hate crimes law.[37] As a look at the course of similar laws in the UK and Canada tells us, we can expect to see all other viewpoints, including Islamic viewpoints, respected and embraced—all except conservative Christianity. Evangelicals and conservative Catholics are simply too "divisive." Too rigid. Too "close-minded."

One way to silence those who stubbornly hold to a belief in absolute truth is to intimidate them. This could actually be the most damaging effect of the coming wave of hate crimes laws. There wouldn't have to be any actual prosecutions under these laws for them to have their intended effect.

It used to be the civil libertarians who were constantly warning about a "chilling effect" on free speech resulting from various exertions of government power. Now the American Civil Liberties Union (ACLU) and similar groups are strangely silent. In fact, when I announced the signing of the Proclamation for Morality, the local chapter of the ACLU let media know that they would be investigating me to see if any state funds had been used in the creation of the proclamation or in the planning of the event.[38] Of course, they found nothing illegal or inappropriate. But one couldn't miss the irony of seeing the self-proclaimed defenders of unpopular speech doing their part to create an atmosphere of intimidation as common citizens prepared to speak out concerning something about which they were passionate.

No matter what the politically correct say, absolute truth still matters. It is the foundation upon which one builds a life of happiness and meaningful contribution. What a waste to spend thousands of dollars renovating an old house but ignoring the fact that its foundation is cracked and crumbling. Many a life is cracking and crumbling because the foundation of absolute truth is being ignored.

Chapter Eight

RECLAIMING CHRISTIAN CONSERVATISM

I<small>N MY FIRST BID FOR REELECTION IN 2006, I DIDN'T EVEN HAVE</small> a Democratic opponent in the general election. I have to confess, that's the fun and low-stress way to campaign for office. But after my remarks about the homosexual agenda and all the media attention surrounding them in 2008, I assumed that might not be the case in the next election. I was correct.

After the session was over in May, the campaign season began, and the Democrats made sure they recruited someone to run against me. This election would be my next challenge and would gauge the effect on voters of the hailstorm of negative media coverage I had endured and of my principle-driven refusal to apologize.

In the 2008 election, my opponent's strategy was to paint me as an extremist who was out of touch with mainstream thinking. He repeatedly pointed to the out-of-context YouTube comments and used them to assert that I must not believe in the Declaration of Independence or the Constitution since I had said that not all lifestyles or religions are equal. I must be quite a clever gal to successfully hide such an un-American ideology through two decades of teaching government in public schools. He also played the "hate speech" card against me.

Thankfully, none of this rang true with the voters—especially those who know me—and thus my opponent's strategy did not work. I won my reelection comfortably with 58 percent of the vote.

I wish I could tell you that my 2010 bid for reelection was easier, but that was not the case. The fact that my opponent was a transgender woman brought national attention to the campaign. Lesbian, gay, bisexual, and transgender (LGBT) publications such as the *Dallas Voice* and *The Advocate* ran online articles commending my opponent and bashing me. The campaign even drew the attention of CNN, which spent two days in Oklahoma City reporting on the race. The *New York Times* ran a story too. Without a doubt, I had more TV and print exposure during the 2010 campaign than I'd had in all the years since I was elected in 2004.

Fortunately, the media coverage did not sway voters against me. I won with 66 percent of the vote. But this and every election remind me I am in office only because the Lord put me here, and I know that the outcome of every campaign is in His hands. From the very beginning of this ordeal, I have taken the position that no political office is worth abandoning my convictions or surrendering to the forces of decay that are weakening our nation. I was, and continue to be, willing to lose an election knowing that I am standing up for what I know is true and right.

I ran the first time by looking people in the eye and unabashedly telling them that I was a conservative Christian and, if elected, would vote like one in the state legislature. The people of District 84 saw fit to send me to the capitol on those terms. If I lose an election at some point in the future, I will happily move on to whatever the next thing is that God has for me. Through the years I've learned to hold whatever God gives me with an open hand.

I serve my state of Oklahoma in the House of Representatives as a Republican, but I want it to be understood that my convictions transcend any party affiliation. Being a Republican has given me the best platform to express my Christian conservative values up to now. If that ever changes, I will change my party affiliation in a heartbeat. When asked why he left the Democratic Party, Ronald Reagan once said, "I didn't leave the Democratic Party. The party left me."[1] As a conservative, Reagan moved to the party that would best allow him to express his values. The same will be true for me if the Republican Party continues to move to the Left politically.

I mention Ronald Reagan because he is regarded as the political leader who resurrected conservatism out of the shambles of liberal philosophy that gained so much political influence in the sixties and seventies. He reminded us of what it means to be conservative and how the principles of conservatism were what guided our Founding Fathers in establishing our original form of government. He applied those principles during his administration and was able to bring this nation back to a position of strength, prosperity, and prominence in the world.

RESTORING THE FOUNDATIONS

At its heart, this book is my attempt to explain why I have made no apology for my stand for the truth of God's Word. I believe very strongly that Christian conservatives need to make no apologies for the values and principles we stand for. Why? Because they work! They bring the most benefits and blessings to the nation that embraces them. Abandoning these principles is one of the many threats to preserving freedom for the future of our great nation. So would you permit an old high school government teacher who misses the classroom a chance to offer you a few thoughts about our amazing system of government and some wisdom from the remarkable men who built it?

There are practical benefits of Christian values that provide for a strong nation and a happy people. These are societal, cultural, and economic benefits—not just spiritual ones. These benefits apply to everyone whether they be a Christian, an atheist, or of another faith tradition. DeWitt Clinton, one of our lesser-known Founding Fathers, once said, "Christianity may be contemplated in two important aspects. First, in reference to its influence on this world; and secondly, in reference to our destiny in the world to come."[2]

In my infamous speech that thrust me into the public spotlight, I mentioned David Barton's booklet *The Practical Benefits of Christianity*, which discusses the five tangible benefits of Christianity for society. Briefly listed, they are (1) a civilized society; (2) a self-governing society; (3) good citizenship; (4) the elevation of science, literature, knowledge, and national stature; and (5) a cohesive value system.[3] Barton's booklet explains each in detail and is an excellent read.

Social conservatives, largely Christians, make up one of three key blocs of conservatives that, together, have allowed the Republican Party to form a majority in the past. The other two are fiscal (economic) conservatives and foreign policy conservatives (strong national defense hawks). Of course, there is considerable overlap among these three groups.

There are some non-Christians among the economic and foreign policy conservatives who dream of crafting a governing majority without the social conservatives, whom they view as a bit of an embarrassment. They are indeed dreaming. I'm convinced that without the passion, energy, civic commitment, and sheer, large numbers of Christians, the Republican Party would be forever doomed to minority status.

The Democratic Party began to jettison social conservative values a long time ago—to the benefit of the Republican Party. The activist base of the party has fully embraced secular humanism and economic socialism. I am a Christian, and I am a conservative, and for now the place I best fit is the Republican Party.

Just what is Christian conservatism? It is a political view based on principles established by the Bible. John Adams wrote in a letter to Thomas Jefferson on June 28, 1813, that "the general Principles, on which the Fathers atchieved [sic] Independence, were...the general Principles of Christianity."[4]

These are principles that never change. They are principles that produce the greatest level of freedom based on individual restraint; in other words, self-government. The more people practice self-control, the less their government has to pass and enforce additional laws. "Of the people, by the people, and for the people" works well only when the people understand they will answer to an authority higher than human government.

The God of the Bible was understood by our Founding Fathers to be that higher authority. God Himself is the author of Christian conservatism and blesses the nations that follow those principles. God is not a Republican, Democrat, Independent, Libertarian, or member of any other political party. It's never a question of, "Is God on our side?" It's always a question of, "Are we on God's side?"

At the end of the Constitutional Convention when Benjamin Franklin was asked about the type of government that had been established, he replied, "A republic, if you can keep it."[5] Our form of government is a republic, not a democracy. A democracy is based on majority rule of the masses. Our Founding Fathers described government by majority rule a mobocracy and did not want it.[6]

Our founders largely recognized the truth that there is a higher law than man's law to which all men are accountable. In our republic, it is the people who are responsible to choose leaders who will uphold the Constitution they established as the law of the land. It is those elected officials who believe they will answer not only to the people but also to God who can best be trusted to uphold the original intent of the Constitution.

One of our Founding Fathers, Noah Webster, published in 1832 his *History of the United States.* In this book he gave advice to school-children on voting. It's a rather lengthy quote, but because it is so rich in its wisdom and so applicable for today, I want to give it in its entirety. He wrote:

> When you become entitled to exercise the right of voting for public officers, let it be impressed on your mind that God commands you to choose for rulers, *just men who will rule in the fear of God.* The preservation of a republican government depends on the faithful discharge of this duty; if the citizens neglect their duty and place unprincipled men in office, the government will soon be corrupted; laws will be made, not for the public good, so much as for selfish or local purposes; corrupt or incompetent men will be appointed to execute the laws; the public revenues will be squandered on unworthy men; and the rights of the citizens will be violated or disregarded. If a republican government fails to secure public prosperity and happiness, it must be because the citizens neglect the divine commands, and elect bad men to make and administer the laws.[7]

Sounds like an editorial hot off the press today. If we were still teaching our children the truths of this statement, one can only imagine what great leaders we might have and the heights to which our nation could rise.

As I speak at churches around the country, I often share the definition of *politics* that appeared in Noah Webster's 1828 *American Dictionary of the English Language.* If we truly want to understand what it means to be a conservative, this definition should be burned upon our hearts and minds, especially those of our elected officials. If it were, the political climate would be drastically different. Webster defined *politics* as:

> The science of government; that part of *ethics* which consists in the regulation and preservation of its safety, peace, and prosperity; comprehending the defense of its existence and rights against foreign control or conquest, the augmentation of its strength and resources, and the protection of its citizens in their rights, *with the preservation and improvement of their morals*. Politics, as a science or an art, is a subject of vast extent and importance [emphasis added].[8]

Oh, that all Americans would live by this definition! Yet the general public can't name the five basic freedoms in the First Amendment. We have politicians who are completely unethical and immoral and who contend that you can't legislate morality. Of course, every time a law is passed, *somebody's* sense of morality is being imposed.

James Madison, our nation's fourth president and the man who is called the "Father of the United States Constitution," in a quotation attributed to him in 1778 said, "We have staked the whole future of American civilization, not upon the power of government, far from it. We have staked the future of all of our political institutions upon the capacity of mankind for self-government; upon the capacity of each and all of us to govern ourselves, to control ourselves, to sustain ourselves according to the Ten Commandments of God."[9]

Sir William Blackstone was the renowned English jurist who was quoted by the Founding Fathers more than any other author except one. In his *Commentaries on the Laws of England* (which sold more copies in America than England), he wrote, "These [laws laid down by God] are the eternal immutable laws of good and evil..."[10]

The further we remove the Ten Commandments from any influence in our society, the more we destroy our nation's foundation. Conservatism today should be all about preserving the intent of our Founding Fathers. They established the Constitution that created these United States. It was written with unchanging principles in mind based on a biblical worldview.

The Pillars of Christian Conservatism

The more I learn about the Bible and our nation's founders, the more conservative I become. Being conservative isn't just a matter of holding a particular opinion on the issues. It's a way of thinking about all of life and government. Our founders recognized that the Bible has two purposes. It is, first and foremost, a book of theology; it is God's revelation to mankind for salvation. But it is also a book of life principles that our founders believed were relevant to all people, even those who did not accept the theology of the Bible.

In the preface to his *American Dictionary of the English Language*, Noah Webster wrote, "In my view, the Christian religion is the most important and one of the first things in which all children, under a free government ought to be instructed.... No truth is more evident to my mind than that the Christian religion must be the basis of any government intended to secure the rights and privileges of a free people."[11] As I mentioned before, conservatism can be broken down into three branches—social, fiscal, and foreign policy—and each one is equally important. You can look at them as the legs on a three-legged stool. Destroy or weaken even one of them, and the stool will not support any weight. Each of these components is rooted in biblical principles and is worth giving a closer look.

Social conservatives want to maintain the moral values upon which our nation was established. The first of these values is written right into the Declaration of Independence: the right to life. The government is responsible to protect life from the moment of conception because in this way we acknowledge that God, not man, is the giver of life. A culture that does not respect God will not respect life and will become a culture of death, much like Nazi Germany under Hitler's rule and Russia during Stalin's reign. In both cases, millions were slaughtered to achieve the twisted vision of men who respected neither God nor the people He created.

Like the sanctity of life, the definition of marriage as the union of one man and one woman is another foundational concept for social conservatives. God established marriage as the base of social order. It is the safe haven for intimate relationships, sexual pleasure, child bearing and rearing, and care for the elderly. As studies have shown, sexual relationships outside biblical marriage have a destabilizing effect on society.

A decade after same-sex marriage was legalized in the Scandinavian countries of Sweden, Denmark, and Norway, the separation between marriage and parenthood had widened. A majority of children in Sweden and Norway were being born out of wedlock, and though the number of homosexual marriages remained steady, traditional marriage showed a steep decline.[12]

Children suffer greatly without the benefit of two parents in a secure, loving environment. Studies in the United States have shown that children from single-parent homes drop out of school at higher rates, get into trouble with the law more often, have more behavioral problems, are more susceptible to drug use, and engage in sexual behavior at earlier ages.[13] This is not the kind of future our children deserve.

It is no wonder our Founding Fathers believed morality and religion were the only hope for our nation's survival. John Adams, our nation's second president, said during an address to the military, "We have no government armed with power capable of contending with human passions unbridled by morality and religion. Avarice, ambition, revenge, or gallantry would break the strongest cords of our Constitution as a whale goes through a net. Our Constitution was made only for a moral and religious people. It is wholly inadequate to the government of any other."[14]

The next leg of conservatism involves fiscal policy. Our Founding Fathers believed that the smaller the government, the more freedom citizens would be able to enjoy. The founders would be appalled to see the number of departments the federal government has created. To them, most of the power was to be vested in states and local governments.

Initially, the federal government was limited to establishing a military for a strong defense, creating courts to uphold federal laws, developing infrastructure, and managing international affairs. The founders did not want the federal government to be involved in education, welfare, labor, banking, or other such issues because they did not want people to become dependent on the government. They believed the greatest amount of freedom was obtained by independence, creativity, hard work, and earned prosperity. Their belief in small government, fewer taxes, and free enterprise has helped make the United States the most prosperous nation in history.

The Bible has a lot to say about hard work and obtaining prosperity through God's favor and blessing. The apostle Paul told the church in Thessalonica, "If anyone isn't willing to work, he should not eat" (2 Thess. 3:10). He also told them to "seek to lead a quiet life, to mind your own business, and to work with your own hands, as we commanded you, so that you may walk properly in the presence of outsiders and not be dependent on anyone" (1 Thess. 4:11–12).

The Ten Commandments also addresses the ownership of property when it says, "Thou shall not steal" and "Thou shall not covet your neighbor's possessions." Christian conservatives believe that our government was established to protect citizens' God-given right to own property. The Declaration of Independence describes this as "the pursuit of happiness." When crafting the Declaration of Independence, Thomas Jefferson drew from Enlightenment philosopher John Locke's belief that everyone has a God-given right to "life, liberty, and estate [ownership of property]."[15] Jefferson changed "estate," or ownership of property, to "pursuit of happiness" to express a broader view of self-actualization.

It is a form of covetousness to take money from those who have worked hard to earn it in order to give it to those who have not earned it. Today that is called spreading the wealth, or income redistribution. The way to spread wealth is to have free markets that allow businesses to develop with limited government intervention. Businesses that provide a quality product or service at a competitive price will grow and succeed; those that don't will close their doors. As businesses grow, they create jobs that make it possible for more people to work, which then grows the economy.

Microsoft founder Bill Gates is a perfect example of this. He started his business with a product and an idea for marketing his newly developed software. He followed through with his plan, and now he has made billions of dollars. In the process he also has helped many others become millionaires and created thousands of jobs worldwide. Automaker Henry Ford and telecommunications pioneer Thomas Edison did the same thing. The best way to help the poor is to give them jobs. Therefore fiscal policy should allow free markets to work in a fair environment. And though social welfare has its place, it should be done through private philanthropists who act according to their free will.

That brings us to the last leg on our stool: foreign policy. All foreign policy should work to protect America's sovereignty. Americans will be free only under the form of government established by our founders and protected by our Constitution. We hear a lot today about globalization and a new world order. Europe has already developed a European Union, and there has been talk about forming a North American Union comprised of Mexico, the United States, and Canada.[16] The danger of these kinds of alliances is that they could impose laws that conflict with our Constitution.

This is one of the major dangers involved in our nation entering into treaties and free trade agreements with other countries. Those documents often include regulations and compromises that, in time, could bring us under international rules. This nation is still "one nation under God." As we enter into more and more international contracts, we may find ourselves giving up more of our sovereignty and becoming less under God and more under the United Nations. I'm with Ronald Reagan when he said, "If we ever forget that we're one nation under God, then we will be a nation gone under."[17]

In the Old Testament God warned Israel not to become like the other nations around them because they had rejected God's ways. Today, the United States has been accused of being behind the times because we, to some extent, still hold to a biblical worldview. We are told we need to catch up with European nations, especially in the area of social policy. The amazing thing is that many Americans are listening to this nonsense. We are the most prosperous nation in the world, and yet we are told we need to change just so we can be better liked throughout the world. We need to maintain our position as a national influencer rather than taking on another country's systems that may not reflect our values.

As a Christian conservative, I believe the principles we hold are the only hope for this nation. They are eternal principles that work for all people and afford everyone the opportunity to achieve the greatest freedom and prosperity. We do not need to apologize for those principles, nor do we need to retreat from them. We have done so in the past and lived to regret it.

Chapter Nine

FROM TYRANNY TO TYRANNY

As a former government teacher and a lover of history, I hope every American knows the story behind the founding of this great nation. With the adoption of the Declaration of Independence on July 4, 1776, the Second Continental Congress declared the colonies free from the tyranny of King George III. By signing that exceptional document, our founders not only cast off Britain's oppressive rule, but they also established America's guiding principles, including the right to life, liberty, and the pursuit of happiness.

From this auspicious beginning emerged one of the greatest nations known to man. We have been blessed not only with prosperity but also with ingenuity and global influence. One would think a nation that escaped tyranny to become a world superpower would never return to oppression, but, sadly, this may not be the case. There are alarming signs that America may now be following in Britain's footsteps and moving toward a new form of tyranny even worse than the one we escaped more than two hundred years ago.

Consider these cases tried recently in the United Kingdom:

- *McFarlane v. Relate Avon Ltd.*: A Christian counselor was dismissed from his job after asking to be exempted from giving sex therapy to homosexual couples. The Employment Appeals Tribunal ruled that his position violated his employer's equal opportunity policy, and his request for an appeal was denied.[1]

- *Masih v. AWAZ Radio*: A Pakistan-born Christian was fired from a volunteer position as host of a Christian radio show after Muslims were offended by his comments during a religious debate. His case was referred to the European Court of Justice to determine whether volunteers are protected by anti-discrimination laws.[2]

- *Ladele v. London Borough of Islington*: A Christian marriage registrar was terminated for not performing civil partnerships for same-sex couples. The court initially supported her claim of religious discrimination, but an appeals court later ruled that her employer did not have to accommodate her religious objections.[3]

- *Eweida v. British Airways*: An appeals court ruled that British Airways could prevent a Christian staff member from wearing a necklace that depicted a cross while allowing Muslim and Hindu employees to wear religious garments. The court ruled this is not discriminatory because Christians generally do not consider wearing crosses a religious requirement.[4] The airline has amended its policy to allow all religious symbols to be worn. In a similar case, *Chaplin v. Royal Devon and Exeter Hospital*, a nurse was reassigned after refusing to stop wearing a crucifix with her uniform. The hospital considered the crucifix a health and safety liability because a disoriented patient might attempt to grab it. Muslims were permitted to wear religious garments.[5]

- *Noah v. Desrosiers trading as Wedge*: A trendy salon was held liable for discrimination after refusing to employ a woman in full Islamic dress.[6] In a separate case, a church was held liable for discrimination after refusing to employ a homosexual youth worker because it was not convinced the man would remain celibate.[7]

- *Glasgow City Council v. McNab*: The court ruled that a Catholic school must employ an atheist to teach religious ethics.[8]

- The Charity Commission of England and Wales ruled that a Catholic adoption agency's religious views did not justify its refusal to place children with homosexual couples. At the time of this decision, it was the only remaining Catholic adoption agency in England and Wales offering adoption services.[9] In a separate case, a Christian couple was barred from being foster parents because their views on homosexuality were considered discriminatory.[10]

How did a nation that transported Christianity to the United States end up in such a place? One need look no farther than the church for answers. In her 2000 book *The C of E: The State It's In*, British author Monica Furlong lamented the steep membership decline in the Church of England. She wrote that the church "is between a rock and a hard place, and there are bitter pills to be swallowed. The most painful fact with which it has to deal...is the all-round drop in numbers:

churchgoers, those on the electoral roles, numbers of baptisms, confirmation, church weddings—all have dropped steadily since the 1930s, with consequential loss both of morals and of income."[11]

Between 1987 and 1996, church attendance among youth ages fourteen to seventeen had dropped 35 percent. Furlong believed that if the trend were to continue, in the next twenty years there would be no youth in the church.[12]

Her warning has proved to be prescient. In his 2009 book *Already Gone*, Ken Ham described a recent visit to a Sunday worship service at an impressive church in London. Although the church had ornate seating to accommodate three thousand people, only a handful of elderly churchgoers sat inside—in chairs set up in the foyer. Ham's observation is consistent with a 2006 Tearfund study that found 66 percent of adults in the United Kingdom have no connection to a church or any other organized religious organization. And the majority of these individuals are not open to attending church in the future.[13]

This trend away from churchgoing is producing a generation of children who are largely ignorant of Christian concepts, according to a 2004 study co-led by Dr. Penny Jennings, a religious education researcher at the University of Wales. In the survey of almost four thousand thirteen- to fifteen-year-old students in Cornwall, England, only 22 percent of the students said they believe in God while 49 percent said they do not. What's more, only 20 percent of the students believed they should obey the Ten Commandments while 52 percent did not.[14] This is not a pretty picture of a nation once known for its dynamic Christian witness.

Today England and much of Europe are better known for their secularism, a belief system that wants to "free" the culture from religious influence. This ideology has become so pervasive that Pope Benedict XVI warned Britons against it during his first state visit there in 2010.

He cautionted them not to embrace "aggressive forms of secularism" that would lead Britain to disregard and even become intolerant of traditional values.[15] If the cases I mentioned earlier are any indication, this is already happening.

UnChristian America?

I would like to believe this loss of faith would never happen in the United States, but current trends suggest there is much cause for concern. Yes, polls show that 92 percent of Americans believe in God and a majority favor having a National Day of Prayer.[16] But when it comes to identifying with a church, Americans are going the way of the British. In its US Religious Landscape Survey, the Pew Forum on Religion and Public Life found that nearly 16 percent of Americans are unaffiliated with a religion. Of that number, a third are under the age of thirty, and 71 percent are under age fifty.[17]

The writings of the majority of America's Founding Fathers show they held the Bible in high regard and believed its principles should be integrated into every area of life. Today, only about a third of American adults believe the Bible is the inspired Word of God and should be taken literally. This figure is down from previous years.[18] Perhaps most troubling is the alarming rate at which youth who were reared in church are dropping out. According to a study by pollster George Barna, six in ten American adults in their twenties are no longer attending church, even though they had been involved during their teen years.[19]

Why is this important? Because if the secularism that has opposed the church in England continues to spread in America, Christianity could lose its influence here too. This could have a dangerous effect on religious liberty. Joseph Story, whom President James Madison appointed to the US Supreme Court in 1811, making him the youngest person to serve as a justice, affirmed this when he wrote, "There is not a truth to be gathered from history, more certain, or more momentous, than this, that civil liberty cannot long be separated from religious liberty without danger, and ultimately without destruction to both. Wherever religious liberty exists, it will, first or last, bring in, and establish political liberty."[20]

The Bible puts it like this: "You will know the truth, and the truth will set you free" (John 8:32). All truth is God's truth and applies not just to spiritual issues but to *all* of life.

In his book *A Christian Manifesto*, noted author Francis Schaeffer warned of a developing clash between secular humanism and biblical Christianity. Schaeffer predicted that as secular humanism gains more and more acceptance in mainstream thinking, a line would be drawn in the sand between secularists and those who hold a biblical worldview. Neither side will be willing to cross it, especially when it comes to social issues such as abortion and same-sex marriage. This resistance to compromise is easy to see in our culture, and Schaeffer predicted it will only get worse as both sides refuse to give up their deeply held convictions.[21]

This is not a battle conservative Christians can ignore because if secularism wins the day, it will radically change this nation. Secular humanism is exactly opposite the view America's founders held. This worldview relies on science and human reason rather than faith and religious values to solve life's problems. Christians who hold a biblical worldview understand that they must depend upon God's guidance and wisdom for daily living.

Liberal theologians have attempted to reconcile secular humanism with the biblical worldview. Invariably, though, the balance of power has come to rest on the side of secular humanism. Since my comments brought me into the public eye, it has been liberal pastors who have come to my office to try to change my point of view.

As we have seen in previous chapters, the call for tolerance will lead only to intolerance of one group: those who stand for the truth of God's Word. These Christians will be labeled bigots, homophobes, xenophobes, hate mongers, and threats to social order. I know. I've been called all of those things.

In November 2009, my husband and two other Oklahoma pastors traveled to Washington DC to join religious leaders from across the country in protesting the recently passed hate crimes bill. The Christian activists gathered outside the Justice Department to express their concern that the law, written to protect homosexuals from "offensive" speech, would be used to silence ministers who preach that homosexuality is a sin. To affirm their free speech rights, several of the pastors preached short sermons presenting the Bible's teaching about homosexuality.

Even more than their sermons, however, the ministers may have made the greatest impact simply by showing up. British attorney Paul Diamond flew from England to Washington at his own expense to congratulate the ministers on their willingness to protest this threat to religious freedom. Diamond defended the Christians in several of the cases I mentioned earlier. He told the pastors in Washington that they were doing exactly what Christians in England should have done ten years earlier when their hate crimes legislation was first gaining ground. If British Christians had spoken up immediately in opposition to the legislation, he believes they could have slowed its progression.

If American Christians don't stand against the godless agenda of secular humanism, we can expect much of the same discrimination British believers have been facing. In fact, there are already signs of an anti-Christian bias at work in the United States.

In 2010, a federal judge stopped the establishment of a constitutional amendment passed by 70 percent of Oklahoma voters. The amendment prohibited the use of Sharia law to decide cases in

Oklahoma courts. Although the strict Islamic law had not been used in Oklahoma courts, voters were alarmed by trends in Britain, where Sharia law is used to decide some civil cases.[22] There is already evidence that Sharia has been considered in cases here in the United States.

In 2009, a Muslim woman in New Jersey was denied a restraining order against her Moroccan ex-husband after he had sexually abused her repeatedly. The family court judge ruled on the grounds that the ex-husband was acting on his religious beliefs about marital rights and not with criminal intent. Fortunately, an appeals court overturned that decision in July 2010, ruling that the judge was "mistaken" to consider the ex-husband's religious beliefs.[23]

This isn't the worst of it, unfortunately. Christian observers have long been concerned about ENDA, or the Employment Non-Discrimination Act, which would prohibit discrimination in hiring on the basis of sexual orientation. The bill was first introduced in 1994 and is now being held until its supporters can drum up enough support to get it passed by Congress and signed into law. Although it is not supposed to apply to churches, religious employers could be forced to hire homosexual applicants even if they don't share the organization's religious convictions or statement of faith. Following his testimony before a Senate committee, Craig Parshall, general counsel for the National Religious Broadcasters, wrote:

> Under ENDA, employers will be subjected to budget-crushing lawsuits, money damages, and the payment of plaintiff's attorney fees for their failure to hire or promote persons because of their sexual orientation, or "gender identity" (read: transgender, transvestite, etc.). I opined in the hearing that the so-called "exemption" for religious groups in ENDA is *more mirage than reality*. Courts have already ruled that religious groups get no

exemption regarding any discrimination that is deemed to be based on "gender," and federal judges have stated that sexual orientation bias is basically a form of "gender discrimination" (rather than a form of "religious" discrimination) under Title VII (the existing employment discrimination law).[24]

At that ENDA hearing in the Senate, Assistant Attorney General Tom Perez linked the bill to the hate crimes law President Obama signed into law on October 28, 2009. He promised an elaborate roll-out of both bills from the Department of Justice.[25] Even as I write, a hate-speech petition filed with the Federal Communications Commission in early 2010, demanding that it investigate conservative radio and TV, is picking up steam.[26] It is supported by a study from the University of California–Los Angeles, which has denounced conservative talk radio for creating "a climate of hate and prejudice."[27]

This thinking isn't limited to researchers at UCLA. In April 2009, the Department of Homeland Security released a report on right-wing extremism. The people it targeted as possible terrorists were described as former military personnel, gun owners, members of groups and organizations that oppose a one-world government, those who reject federal authority in favor of state or local authority, and single-issue voting groups who oppose abortion or illegal immigration.[28] These "extremists" could be any number of Christians I know who would never attempt to harm anyone. They simply share the same concerns that I do about our nation's drift away from its conservative Christian roots.

This report caused such a huge uproar that it was pulled almost immediately, but that doesn't mean the government has changed its mind about the document's findings. It will surface again if government officials remain in power who think conservative and Christian beliefs make a person dangerous.

THE STONING OF SALLY KERN

ENCROACHING LIBERALISM

Opposition to conservative Christian viewpoints is nothing new, and the judicial system has been a key battleground. Prayers have been banned at graduations[29] and football games,[30] and Christian groups have been denied recognition as campus clubs[31]—all because of acts of the courts. This is because more and more activist judges are being appointed who make laws rather than interpret them.

These judges do not care about the original intent of the framers of the Constitution. In their liberal thinking, it is acceptable to decide cases based on their personal political and philosophical views instead of what the Constitution actually says and means. This was a danger our Founding Fathers anticipated. Thomas Jefferson wrote in 1819 that "the Constitution...is a mere thing of wax in the hands of the judiciary, which they may twist, and shape into any form they please."[32]

This judicial activism became prevalent in the early twentieth century around the same time humanists began gaining influence. The attitude of these judges was summarized clearly by Associate Supreme Court Justice Oliver Wendell Holmes Jr., who helped promote this mind-set. He said, "The felt necessities of the time, the prevalent moral and political theories...even the prejudices of which judges share with their fellow-men, have had a good deal more to do than the syllogism [legal reasoning process] in determining the rules by which men should be governed."[33]

Did you read anything in that statement about the Constitution? Not at all. The Constitution has little meaning to judges like Justice Holmes. They make decisions based on their experiences and societal norms. As activist judges continue to be appointed who are not favorable to the Judeo-Christian worldview, Christians will be hard pressed to receive justice in the courts.

Alexander Hamilton, another of our Founding Fathers, had a

view of the courts that was totally different from Justice Holmes's. This is evident in his 1788 comments in *The Federalist Papers*. He said in "Federalist No. 78," "Whoever attentively considers the different departments of power must perceive, that, in a government in which they are separated from each other, the judiciary, from the nature of its functions, will always be the least dangerous to the political rights of the Constitution; because it will be least in a capacity to annoy or injure them."[34] Many a ruling from the federal judicial system has caused much annoyance and injury to those of us who believe decisions should be based on the original intent of the Constitution.

The attack on Christian conservatism is happening not only in the courts. The Federal Communications Commission (FCC) wields significant power to regulate what is broadcast over the radio and television, and some liberals would love to use the commission to muzzle conservative viewpoints. In recent years there have been attempts to resurrect the Fairness Doctrine, which required broadcasters to devote airtime to opposing viewpoints. The doctrine was abolished in 1987 on the grounds that it violated freedom of speech on the airways, but those on the liberal side would love to see the Fairness Doctrine reinstated in order to silence conservative talk radio and television networks such as Fox News.[35] They realize this is not going to happen anytime soon, so liberals want to dispose of these conservative whistleblowers through regulations.[36]

Just the possibility of this happening can be intimidating to broadcasters. Since I stumbled into the media spotlight in 2008, not one Christian television station has interviewed me. I have been attacked by news pundit Keith Olbermann on MSNBC, mocked by Ellen DeGeneres on her television show, and contacted by the *Dr. Phil Show* about participating in a discussion panel on his program. Liberal commentator Alan Colmes has interviewed me twice on his radio program. Much to my surprise and relief, he was very fair and a perfect gentleman.

I continue to be maligned all over the Internet and on YouTube, but Christian television will not touch me. Fortunately, that has not been the case with Christian radio. Radio show hosts such as Dick Bott of Bott Radio Network and Tony Perkins of the Family Research Council have shown me a great deal of support on their programs.

What is the problem? Many Christian broadcasters purposely avoid controversial subjects because they fear lawsuits, verbal attacks by activist organizations, possible FCC sanctions, and, it's sad to say, they don't want to offend viewers who think Christians shouldn't be involved in sociopolitical issues. They just don't seem to realize that now is the time to speak out. I have said many times, "It is time to wake up and speak up!" The church and Christian broadcasters need to get this message.

Secularists aren't shying away from indoctrinating our culture with their atheistic, humanist worldview. In 2009 the University of Oklahoma celebrated the one-hundred-fiftieth anniversary of Charles Darwin's birth and the one-hundredth anniversary of the publishing of his book on evolutionary theory, *On the Origins of the Species*. This was a grave concern to many Christians in Oklahoma. After all, Oklahoma is the most churched state in the country and the reddest state politically.

Richard Dawkins, the world-famous atheist from England, was invited to speak as part of the yearlong celebration. I am pleased to say that Dawkins declined to accept an honorarium because there was such an outcry by Christian taxpayers that public funds would be used to pay a man who angrily opposes the faith of most Oklahomans. However, that was only a partial victory. So many students responded to his visit that the event had to be moved to a larger facility. Roughly three thousand faculty, students, and community members attended the speech, and Dawkins received several standing ovations and excited rounds of applause. After hearing that report, I was reminded once again that the teaching of evolution in our schools is having a far greater impact on the way the next generation thinks than the church is willing to admit.

The decline of religion among young people is becoming a trend in America faster than what we would like to believe. Why are kids dropping out of church? Because the church often fails to provide acceptable answers to their questions. They are turning instead to atheist teachers who offer them something new. This has to change.

These trends should sound forth an alarming wake-up cry to Christians that the secular humanist agenda is an unfeigned and odious threat to our religious liberty. We don't want to follow England down the path to a new tyranny, when for more than two hundred years we have experienced the blessings of freedom. Are we willing, like our Founding Fathers, to "pledge to each other our Lives, our Fortunes and our sacred Honor"[37] to preserving our republic? The benefit would be not only for ourselves but also for our children, grandchildren, and all future generations.

Chapter Ten

THE WAR AT SCHOOL

SINCE I BECAME A STATE REPRESENTATIVE, I'VE OFTEN challenged evangelical Christians who claim to be Bible-believing conservatives to stand for what we believe and reclaim our place as the protectors of freedom in our nation. I've discovered as I have spoken to churches all over Oklahoma that God's people don't really understand the severity of the liberal push to undermine our nation's Christian foundations or what the ramifications will be if they succeed.

As I've shared my story, God has impressed upon many that we are, indeed, in a cultural war and that it is time for Christians to put on the armor of God and stand for truth. Actually, it is past time to become engaged in this battle. Much ground already has been lost. Only by the grace of God will we be able to overcome and reclaim the moral ground that has been taken.

In her wonderful book *Total Truth*, Nancy Pearcey does a superb job of showing how faith has been relegated to what she calls the second floor of living. She likens truth claims to a two-story building. On the first floor are "facts," empirical data, science, and reason. On the second floor are subjective opinions and beliefs that can be neither proved nor disproved.[1] In our contemporary culture, it's OK for Christians to practice their faith as long as they keep it on the second floor, or, in other words, to themselves. They're told faith is a private matter. No wonder our society is so decadent. The truth we need to restrain people's passions is absent except in Christians' private lives.

Sadly, many Christians have swallowed this false doctrine. I call it the "unless concept." They believe Christians are to seek first the kingdom of God (see Matthew 6:33) *unless* they work in government. They think believers are to acknowledge God in all their ways and allow Him to direct their path (see Proverbs 3:5–6) *unless* they are elected officials. In effect, this kind of thinking causes Christians to pretend that they do not have any convictions in certain circumstances. But what good are convictions if we don't live by them every day and in all situations?

A classic example of this compartmentalizing of faith took place one day in my office at the capitol. I don't remember the specific issue being discussed, but I do vividly recall my fellow representative's words that day. He said, "Sally, this isn't Sunday school. It doesn't work like that here."

I knew this man to be a fine Christian and very active in his church, so I could hardly believe my ears. My reply was, "I know this isn't Sunday school, but biblical principles apply anywhere."

It's no accident that so many people have come to believe this "unless concept." The idea that Christians can't express their faith in the public square has been stealthily woven into the fabric of our society for years, primarily through our public education system. I know some people will cringe over this statement, but please bear with me while I explain what I mean.

Merriam-Webster's Collegiate Dictionary defines *stealthy* as "slow, deliberate and secret in action and character, intended to escape observation." Secular humanists want to shift our society away from a biblical worldview, and their method has been nothing short of deliberate and intentional.

In his book *Whoever Controls the Schools Rules the World*, Gary DeMar says, "Whoever controls the educational system will set the goals for the nation, define and establish its moral values, and ultimately rule the future in every area of life."[2] His statement is not unlike the popular quote, "The philosophy of the schoolroom in one generation will be the philosophy of government in the next."[3] These statements point to something we know intrinsically: those who control the educational system in America wield incredible influence over the next generation of citizens. This is why we must understand what those who influenced our modern educational system taught and believed.

SOCIAL ENGINEERING

Philosopher John Dewey is considered the "father of progressive education," a movement that began in the late nineteenth century and attempted to center education around students' experiences rather than focusing primarily on disseminating a preestablished set of facts.

The curriculum that grew out of this movement shared Dewey's skepticism of religion and traditional values, as well as his view of evolution as a fundamental truth. Later leaders in progressive education would employ techniques from the field of behavioral psychology that trained children in order to elicit certain desired responses, much as animals were taught to do in research labs.

Dewey was a humanist and a signer of the 1933 *Humanist Manifesto*, the first of three documents that have outlined the humanist worldview. He considered socialism superior to capitalism and believed schools were vehicles through which social reform should take place. In his 1899 book *The School and Society*, Dewey wrote, "The mere absorption of facts and truth is so exclusively individual an affair that it tends very naturally to pass into selfishness."[4] In his book *My Pedagogic Creed*, Dewey said he believed "the social life of the child is the basis of concentration, or correlation, in all his training or growth."[5] He argued that the school "is primarily a social institution," writing that "examinations are of use only so far as they test the child's fitness for social life."[6]

In other words, Dewey is saying that teaching historical facts and empirical data is not as important as promoting a student's social development. This is what I meant when I said in my infamous speech that schools are not teaching facts and knowledge anymore but rather are indoctrinating students.

Dewey's books became mandatory reading in teacher training colleges, as did Benjamin Bloom's *Taxonomy of Educational Objectives*. Like Dewey, Bloom was concerned with more than students' knowledge of empirical facts. It is evident from Bloom's educational philosophy that he wanted to shape students' values and attitudes. He wrote in his 1981 book *All Our Children Learning* that "the purpose of education and the schools is to change the thoughts, feelings, and actions of students."[7] My guess is that most parents think the purpose of education is to teach subjects such as history, English, and math.

This idea that schools could be used as agents for social reform didn't stop with Dewey and Bloom. Behavioral psychologist B. F. Skinner argued against the concept of free will and claimed that behavioral outcomes could be controlled with the right social engineering. In his 1971 book *Beyond Freedom and Dignity*, he wrote that man "plays two roles: one as a controller, as the designer of a controlling culture, and another as the controlled, as the products of a culture."[8]

When I said in my speech that we are turning out learners rather than thinkers, this is what I was referring to. Our educational system is turning out products for the job market, not people who can think critically. This emphasis is evident in the federal School-to-Work program, which recommends that students begin exploring possible careers no later than seventh grade and decide on a career path by the eleventh grade. This choice determines their courses through their high school years.[9] Most of the twelfth-graders I taught didn't know what they wanted to do with their lives. How in the world do we expect younger students to know?

Dewey, Bloom, and Skinner all were atheists whose philosophy of education still influences our educational system today. They each thought religion was useless and that it merely shackled human intellect. Education, in their view, was the means to purge religion from students. Their influence is still evident in an educational model called Outcome-Based Education, which tends to be popular among liberal reformers who think education needs to be fundamentally restructured.

Many of the "outcomes" in this educational approach concern attitudes, values, and opinions rather than objective facts. This educational approach seeks to do more than teach; it seeks to conform students' beliefs and behavior to an established set of social norms.

Today, the National Education Association (NEA) and its state-level affiliates are carrying out Dewey's, Bloom's, and Skinner's vision for education as a social change agent. At the NEA's national convention in 2009, the teachers passed a five-point plan that advanced homosexuality and same-sex marriage. Point one encouraged its union counterparts to support state legislation that registers same-sex couples as if they were married. Point two built on point one, claiming it doesn't matter whether the relationship between homosexual couples is called marriage, civil unions, or domestic partnerships as long as it is treated on par with traditional marriage.

In point three, the NEA promised that state affiliates would have their support in opposing state laws or constitutional amendments that created any distinction between heterosexual and homosexual couples. Point four called for the repeal of the Defense of Marriage Act (DOMA), a federal law that defines marriage as the union of one man and one woman, while point five recognized the First Amendment right of churches not to perform same-sex marriages.[10] I guess this last point was to give the appearance that they respect religious freedom.

Lost in these politically correct education objectives is actual learning. As studies have shown, our children are suffering from lower test scores, higher illiteracy rates,[11] and increased violence in schools.[12]

An underlying theme in modern education is that children are "sick" when they come to school and need to be cured. What ails them? A horrible disease called "parental influence."[13] According to Chester Pierce, professor of education and psychology at Harvard University, "Every child who enters school at the age of five is mentally ill because he enters school with an allegiance toward our elected officials, our founding fathers, our institutions, the preservation of this form of government that we have, patriotism, nationalism, sovereignty. All this proves that the children are sick, because a truly well individual is one who has rejected all of those things, and is what I would call the true international child of the future."[14] Parents, did you think you were the only ones who had dreams for your children's future?

RADICAL REVISIONISM

According to historian David Barton, regardless of the subject being taught, Christian principles and Bible verses were once woven throughout our nation's textbooks, even in math word problems.[15] This is hardly the case today. You won't find social studies lessons like this one titled "Origin of Civil Society and Government" from an 1867 public school textbook: "Why do men live together in society? Because God made them to live together in society.... Is there any higher law than the Constitution? The Constitution is the highest human law; but the law of God is the highest of all laws."[16]

From 1690 until the late 1700s, the *New England Primer* was the most popular textbook used in colonial schools. It taught the alphabet using truths from the Bible and contained a short catechism of one hundred seven questions designed to teach students right from wrong, and other moral truths. Today religion has been stripped from America's public school textbooks, as New York University psychology professor Paul Vitz has documented.

In a study of sixty social studies textbooks that were used by more than 85 percent of public school students, he found that not one discussed the spiritual motivation behind the Pilgrims' journey to America. Vitz wrote of his findings, "Are public school textbooks biased? Are they censored? The answer to both is yes. And the nature of the bias is clear: Religion, traditional family values, and conservative political and economic positions have been reliably excluded from children's textbooks."[17]

After TV talk show host Ellen DeGeneres played the audio clips of my speech, she and her audience got quite a laugh when they heard me say that schools today are not teaching facts and knowledge but are indoctrinating students. I wonder if they would laugh if they had heard Shirley McCune, then senior director of the Mid-Continent Regional Educational Laboratory, say at the 1989 Governor's Conference on Education that "what we are about is the total restructuring of our society.... We no longer see the teaching of facts and information as the primary outcome of education."[18]

One of the goals of this "total restructuring" is to replace our Judeo-Christian ethic with one based on secular humanism. This shift has been taking place for some time, and the education system long has been seen as a strategic partner. In his 1930 book *Humanism: A New Religion*, humanist minister Charles F. Potter wrote that education "is thus a most powerful ally of humanism, and every American school is a school of humanism. What can a theistic Sunday school's meeting for an hour once a week and teaching only a fraction of the children do to stem the tide of the five-day program of humanistic teaching?"[19]

This indoctrination is easy to see in the colleges that train teachers. Today some programs are giving a sociopolitical litmus test for future educators. The University of Minnesota oversees a program called the Teacher Education Redesign Initiative. In a 2009 draft report, its Race, Culture, Class, and Gender Task Group proposed requiring every faculty member who trains teachers to "comprehend and commit to the centrality of race, class, culture, and gender issues in teaching and learning, and consequently, frame their teaching and course foci accordingly."[20]

Aspiring teachers would be taught to do the same, and to understand and accept that they are either privileged or oppressed. In order to build their "cultural intelligence," education students would be required to become well-versed in such issues as "white privilege," "institutional racism," and the "myth of meritocracy in the United States." The task group recommended that "non-performing" students, or those who don't fall in ideolgoical lockstep, undergo a remedial reeducation process.[21]

Basically, this is a heavy does of social justice education, which conservative commentator David Horowitz defines as "shorthand for opposition to American traditions of individual justice and free market economics."[22] He goes on to say this ideology teaches students that "American society is an inherently 'oppressive' society that is 'systemically' racist, sexist, and classist and thus discriminates institutionally against women, non-whites, working Americans, and the poor."[23]

William Ayers, a former education professor at the University of Illinois–Chicago, is considered a leader in promoting social justice concepts in our nation's classrooms. If you know anything about Ayers, you know that he is a good friend of President Obama as well as a former leader of the radical left Weather Underground organization. During the sixties and seventies, the group protested American "imperialism" by organizing a campaign of bombings against several public buildings, including the Pentagon. Ayers was never convicted of any crimes, but he told the *New York Times* in 2001, "I don't regret setting bombs.... I feel we didn't do enough."[24]

After his Weather Underground days, Ayers became an educator and has spoken openly of his desire to use public schools to train a generation of revolutionaries who will overturn America's oppressive, capitalistic regime.[25] Perhaps now you can understand why we have so many teachers who are anti-American and believe that this great nation is an oppressive, greedy, war-mongering whore.

What is sad in all this is that many of those coming out of the universities that teach these concepts don't really understand the perverted nature of what they have been taught. They haven't connected the dots because, after all, we are supposed to love and care for those who are less fortunate and have faced injustice, poverty, and discrimination. This is what good people think, and, of course, it is what the Bible teaches. But the Bible also teaches that individuals and churches, not the government, are to love and care for the oppressed. We are to do it from a willing and loving heart, not from coercion by the government.

Education, as it currently exists in America, is more about changing our students than it is about educating them. It is being used to mold youth into global citizens rather than patriotic Americans. It is being used to disconnect students from any traditional values they may have received from their parents. It is promoting tolerance based upon the absence of absolute truth. And this has been happening gradually right under our noses.

This was not what our Founding Fathers envisioned as the purpose of education. In his DVD *Four Centuries of American Education*, historian David Barton documents how the original purpose of education was to teach religion, morality, and knowledge. This foundation has been deteriorating ever since John Dewey introduced his atheistic, socialistic ideas into our education system.

RELIGION, SCHOOLS, AND FREE SPEECH

Today's textbooks contain much revisionist history based upon what progressive education elites want us to think. This is why so many Americans believe the vast majority of our nation's founders were deists or atheists who wrote a constitution void of religious influence. While it is true that our founders wanted to separate the institutions of church and state, that was not an attempt to remove religious influence from government or the public square. It was to prevent the church from controlling government and the government from controlling the church.

Most Americans have never heard of Fisher Ames, but he was a congressman from Massachusetts who served in the first US Congress, which was the group of legislators who wrote the Bill of Rights. During debates about the wording of the First Amendment, Ames made a motion that it say, "Congress shall make no law establishing religion, or to prevent the free exercise thereof, or to infringe the rights of conscience."[26] His motion was adopted, but the language was further revised to eventually state, "Congress shall make no law respecting an establishment of religion, or prohibiting the free exercise thereof; or abridging the freedom of speech, or of the press;

or the right of the people peaceably to assemble, and to petition the Government for a redress of grievances."[27]

If anyone ought to know what the First Amendment says about religion in our schools, it's the man who helped craft the Establishment Clause. In *Palladium* magazine on September 20, 1789, Ames stated, "We have a dangerous trend beginning to take place in our education. We're starting to put more and more textbooks into our schools.... We've become accustomed of late of putting little books into the hands of children containing fables and moral lessons.... We are spending less time in the classroom on the Bible, which should be the principal text in our schools.... The Bible states these great moral lessons better than any other manmade book."[28]

Ames had no problem with the Bible in public schools. Yet today a teacher can't even have a Bible on his desk without being challenged by administrators.[29]

President John Quincy Adams didn't have a problem with the Bible in schools either. In an 1811 letter written to his son from St. Petersburg, Russia, where he was serving as an ambassador, Adams wrote, "It is essential, my son...that you should form and adopt certain rules or principles, for the government of your own conduct and temper....It is in the Bible, you must learn them, and from the Bible how to practice them. Those duties are to God, to your fellow-creatures, and to yourself."[30] And Patrick Henry, the great champion of liberty, said of the Bible: "Here...is a book worth more than all the other books that were ever printed."[31]

Today students have to file lawsuits in order to exercise their First Amendment right to start a Bible club in their school. Think that sounds like alarmist right-wing propaganda? Think again. This happened in 2009 in the Lindenhurst school district on Long Island. Although the district denied any wrongdoing, it agreed to settle the lawsuit out of court and paid the students' $2,500 legal fees.[32]

To add insult to injury, every time the United States pays dues to the United Nations Educational, Scientific and Cultural Organization (UNESCO), we are helping to further anti-morality, anti-marriage, and anti-American ideas into our education system. UNESCO entered into a contract in 2004 with Microsoft Corporation to write a "master curriculum" for teacher training in information technologies that will "form the basis for deriving training content to be delivered to teachers."[33] Developing worldwide curricula reflecting UNESCO values is one of the goals of this endeavor. I don't know about you, but I want American teachers to promote American goals and values.

UNESCO is also developing guidelines for teaching sex education, with abstinence until marriage as only one of many choices young people should consider. UNESCO guidelines outline teaching five- through eight-year-old children masturbation along with tolerance for same-sex couples and people of different sexual orientations.[34] Between the ages of nine and fifteen, children are taught even more about specific sex-related practices, such as orgasms and abortions.[35] I won't shock you any further, but is it any wonder that our children can't concentrate on learning when they're being turned into sex-crazed young people?

My opponents accuse me of wanting to turn our nation into a theocracy. I merely want to reclaim the republic that was established by men such as Fisher Ames, John Adams, Patrick Henry, George Washington, Thomas Jefferson, John Winthrop, and Noah Webster. Each of these Founding Fathers spoke often of the Bible and the principles it espoused. They were never accused of creating a theocracy.

Our educational system has been the tool to undermine our nation's faith and values and lead us down a dangerous path toward secularism. Sadly, too few parents, legislators, *and churches* are aware of what's happening—all to the peril of our children and America's future.

Conclusion

FALL BACK? NOT HARDLY

W HAT A SICKENING CESSPOOL OF HATE AND FEAR CHRIS-
tianity has become. How can so many of its adherents live
with themselves, when they actively take steps to bully, victimize, and
bring misery to the lives of a group of people for the sole crime of
being different?"[1]

These are the words of a blogger named "Martin" posted on a
website titled, "The Atheist Experience." I'm always saddened and a
little angered when I read sentiments like the above, because I know
that the reality of Christianity is starkly different from that bitter and
accusatory characterization.

Sadly, a growing number of people in America have a similar opinion, and many of them are young people, the future of our
nation. A constant theme in many of the e-mails I received was "when
you and those your age are gone, we will have equality because the
younger generation will be more tolerant."

As we have seen on the previous pages, the liberal, more "progressive" America they long for will not be the utopia of tolerance and
freedom they've convinced themselves it will be. Quite the contrary.

What the last few generations of Americans don't understand is that most of what they love and value about America is a gift from earlier generations—generations that held tightly to values and beliefs that our contemporaries have come to despise. They're living off the capital bequeathed to them by those forerunners, and that resource is running desperately low.

Like the atheist blogger Martin's accusations, there is an up-is-down, left-is-right backwardness about the arguments I hear from homosexual activists and their philosophical allies. Christians are accused of being mean and heartless, when the reality is, the lion's share of charitable giving, serving, and helping is done by people of faith in this country. Churchgoing folks are characterized as joyless and miserable. And yet numerous studies have shown that people who attend church regularly and pray are happier, healthier, and more content as a whole than those who don't.[2]

That same bizarre backwardness has been the case with many of the accusations and allegations made against my husband and me in this conflict. Consider the following:

Several of the homosexual activist websites have carried reports of rumors that my husband was a member of the KKK when we lived in Idaho. That is, of course, a lie. The truth is that he is the pastor, by choice, of an inner-city church with a multiracial congregation and with a number of wonderful African American individuals on staff and with ministry outreaches that directly focus help and hope on neighborhoods and communities that are predominantly non-white.

As people who adhere to a biblical view of sexual morality, we've been caricatured in countless articles and Internet comment threads as being busybodies who obsess over the sexual practices of others, without regard to personal privacy. And yet it is our son who has been the target of rampant, erroneous, and hurtful speculation about his private life at the hands of these same activists.

As conservatives, we've been the target of typical liberal stereo-typing as rich, greedy Republicans living in an insular country club world and with no concern for the poor or the oppressed. The reality is that we live in a working-class neighborhood and my husband leads a church that is second to none in Oklahoma City in providing real, compassionate service to the struggling and the hurting. Ministries at Olivet Baptist include a food pantry, a clothing ministry, a health clinic, kids camps for inner-city children, a homeless men's shelter, housing for homeless women with children, literacy programs, and dozens of other initiatives.

Most ironically—given that we are supposed to be filled with hate and revulsion for people who have lived the homosexual lifestyle—is that we serve as a host location for First Stone Ministries, a wonderful organization whose purpose is "to lead the sexually and relationally broken into a liberating relationship with Jesus Christ as Savior and Lord" with a "detailed emphasis on overcoming all forms of sexual brokenness including homosexuality, sexual abuse and addiction to pornography."[3] We also help operate an HIV/AIDS clinic in which testing, counseling, and referral for treatment are offered at no cost.

On and on it goes. Sometimes it seems as if most of the horrible things that are being said about me are not simply untrue; they are the *opposite* of what is true. It is one thing to be falsely accused of hate when one is actually indifferent. It is more hurtful to be accused of hate when you know there is only love in your heart.

My stand was against the homosexual political agenda, not individuals. I respect all human beings as those made in the image of God with the freedom to choose their own path to follow. My husband and I pray every night that God would lead homosexuals to wholeness in Jesus Christ. We pray for some specifically by name. God loves homosexuals, and so do I. They need our love and understanding.

In spite of all this, I have refused to apologize and back down from my beliefs. And so the attacks continue.

Take Tim Gill, for example. He is the software multimillionaire homosexual activist I mentioned in my now-famous speech and in earlier chapters of this book. Gill has personally given more than $150 million toward homosexual causes and political candidates and has organized other ultra-wealthy homosexuals into a strategic funding cartel called "The Cabinet." Previously Gill has stated that "his mission is to 'punish the wicked'—meaning those who stand in the way of his long-range political strategy to advance the homosexual agenda."[4]

I harbor no doubts that he included little Sally Kern among those "wicked" they want eliminated when he spoke at the Gay, Lesbian, Bisexual, Transgender Caucus meeting held at the Democratic National Convention in Denver in 2008. In that eight-minute address Gill called me out by name twice and referred to himself as a "career counselor." By that he meant that he planned to help people like me find another line of work by defeating us in the next election. You too are part of the wicked in the eyes of Gill and his allies if you happen to believe that marriage is only between one man and one woman and are willing to say so publicly.

It's a worn-out phrase; nevertheless, we are indeed in a *cultural war*. And it is past time to become engaged in this battle. Much ground has already been lost and claimed by the homosexual activists. But it is not too late to reverse that damage to our culture and bring restoration.

My hope is that my story has inspired and motivated you to join the ranks with those of us who are fighting the homosexual agenda and the war to preserve marriage. Or perhaps your battlefield is broken homes, human sex trafficking, drug and alcohol addiction, the morally bankrupt education system, pornography, or any other area where turmoil, hopelessness, and personal destruction are evident in people's lives. Traditional marriage, as the most basic unit of society, is inextricably linked to every battle that is raging in people's lives today. It is like the hub of a wheel. If the hub is destroyed, the entire wheel will fall apart. If marriage is redefined into meaninglessness, then, like a rock thrown into a pond, the ripples will affect every corner of our society.

JOIN THE RANKS

I want to bring this all together to show you the part you can personally play in this battle. But before I mention specific ways to engage in the culture war, I need to make sure you're ready to engage the enemy. No branch of the military sends soldiers into battle without first putting them through boot camp in order to prepare them as much as possible for what lies ahead.

If you choose to accept this mission, you must first take a long, hard look at your own life. Second Corinthians 13:5 says, "Examine yourselves to see whether you are in the faith; test yourselves" (NIV). Are you in the faith? While many people are doing lots of wonderful things to positively impact hurting people's lives, only those who are doing it through the power of the Holy Spirit will reap an eternal reward both for themselves and others. We cannot confront the evil in the world today in our own strength.

Joining the ranks of the people of faith is as easy as A-B-C. First, you have to *acknowledge* that all have sinned and fall short of the glory of God. No matter how good a person you might be, compared to God's Son, Jesus, we all fall short. Next you must *believe* in Jesus as the One who took your sins upon Himself and put them to death on the cross of Calvary. This believing is more than just a mental assent. It is a commitment that involves turning control of your life over to

THE STONING OF SALLY KERN

Him who created you and letting Him accomplish His purpose in your life.

Last, you must be willing to *confess* your sins and *commit* your life to Him. Only after you learn the A-B-Cs can your life take on deeper purpose and become richer than you ever imagined.

Like any good soldier, you must be willing to study your training manual, the Bible. Just imagine the catastrophes that would occur on the battlefield if soldiers never read and applied the information found in their war manual. The Bible contains the "unsearchable riches of Christ" (Eph. 3:8, NIV), and we can never discover all of the truth and wisdom found within its pages.

Finally, you will need to connect to a group of people who share your desire to study and practice the principles found in the Bible. You will need their support. Every soldier knows he is the most vulnerable when he is separated from his unit.

As we have seen throughout this book, this battle is one that is largely being fought in the political sphere and at the state and local level. Therefore it is imperative that you become an informed voter and support true conservative candidates who will uphold the moral principles of our Founding Fathers. Notice that I said you must become an informed voter. This means you will have to educate yourself on the issues and the candidates. Every political party has county and state organizations you can join to discuss the important issues, both national and local.

If there isn't a conservative political forum in your area, then start one. It's easier than you think. My husband and I helped to start one in 2009 with friends we met regularly with at the local gun range. We ate lunch together before we went out to shoot, and we always engaged in some lively political discussions. Soon this group of five became ten, then twenty, then thirty. The next thing we knew, we had to gather in one of the conference rooms because our little group of friends was getting so large.

Our discussions continued to be not only lively but also very informative. Soon, a few local and state elected officials began attending. They were always given the opportunity to talk about what was happening at city hall, the county commissioner's office, or the state capitol. During the 2010 election season we invited candidates to come talk about their campaigns. We had those running for Oklahoma governor show up, as well as the candidates for Congress, the state legislature, and other state-level offices.

The impact we were having was being felt all across central Oklahoma, and people continued to join this group of concerned citizens. Today, roughly one hundred people meet every Friday for what we call the High Noon Club. Those who attend not only have become better informed citizens, but also they often go to the state capitol to talk with their representative or senator about the issues that are most important to them.

If you don't personally know your elected officials, I encourage you to go meet them and then visit them from time to time. They need to know that you are watching them and the way they vote; after all, they work for you.

It also is important that you support candidates you believe in by contributing to their campaigns with sweat equity and financial resources. This will put you in a select group: the few who actually get involved. Candidates are always looking for volunteers. You can also run for office yourself, especially for a local position on the school board, library commission, or city council. A true conservative at this level can have a tremendous effect on policy and help turn back the tide of socialism that is encroaching upon our freedoms. Remember, I had never seriously considered running for office before 2002. If a little ole grandmother can do it, so can you.

STAND AND BE COUNTED

There is an illustration I use when speaking to groups that really gets an important point across about how detached and disconnected many good people have become from this vital area of political knowledge and involvement. I got the idea for this exercise from the book *Stand and Be Counted* by Robert Dugan.

I begin by asking everyone in the room to stand. (Please imagine you're standing as you begin to answer these same questions.) Then I say, "As long as you know the answer to each question, continue to stand. Once you don't know an answer, sit down. Once you sit down, you cannot stand back up." I encourage everyone to be absolutely honest. You'll have to be on your honor.

The first question is: Who's the president of the United States? I've never lost anyone on that question.

Second question: Who's your governor? Often a few sit down here.

Third question: Who's your senior United States senator? Again, some sit down.

Fourth question: Who's your junior United States senator? A few more sit down.

Fifth question: Who's your United States congressional representative? More drop out here.

Sixth question: Who's your state senator? Now lots of people sit down.

Seventh question: Who's your state representative? Even more sit down.

At this point, there is often no one left standing. Sometimes a handful might still be. Are you still standing in your mind? At this point, the rest of the audience usually applauds the few, if any, who are still standing. And they should, but then I remind them there is one more question.

The final question is: Have you prayed for these seven people by name in the last seven days? If not, please sit down. Unfortunately, if there were any people left standing before this question, they almost always sit down.

Then I quote 1 Timothy 2:1–4: "First of all, then, I urge that petitions, prayers, intercessions, and thanksgivings be made for everyone, for kings and all those who are in authority, so that we may lead a tranquil and quiet life in all godliness and dignity. This is good, and it pleases God our Savior, who wants everyone to be saved and to come to the knowledge of the truth."

The hard fact is, most good people don't have any idea who the seven elected officials are who have significant influence over them at the state and national levels. Praying for your elected leaders is commanded by God. It is not an option. And nothing is mentioned about whether or not you voted for them or even like them.

This passage of Scripture does more than just command us to pray for our leaders. It tells us *why* we should pray for them: "so that we may lead a tranquil and quiet life in all godliness and dignity." Sadly, the world is too often a war zone in our streets, schools, and neighborhoods—and sometimes even within our own homes. Is it any wonder that this is the case when most Christians don't even know who their elected officials are, let alone pray for them?

The cultural war is at a feverish pitch, and most people don't even know it's going on. They are MIA—missing in action. As long as their lives are not directly impacted, they couldn't care less. They want the blessing but not the battle. The peace but not the pressure. The comfort but not the cross. Does this describe you?

George Washington once said, "The propitious smiles of Heaven, can never be expected on a nation that disregards the eternal rules of order and right, which Heaven itself has ordained."[5] Our world has recklessly disregarded absolute truth; nevertheless, it is unknowingly crying out for Christians to champion the eternal rules of order and right. Yet we sit idly by just playing church, too often ignoring God's eternal rules ourselves.

We all need the smile of heaven to shine down upon us.

I for one have determined to do my part to speak out for what is right in the sight of God—to expose the liberal attacks on Christian conservatism by those who would unravel the moral fabric of our nation and thereby compromise the future.

My prayer is that the stand I have taken in my little corner of the world will challenge others to do the same wherever they are in the world. I pray this will be done in a spirit of love that overcomes judgmentalism and condemnation out of a genuine concern for future generations. For this reason I will not apologize for saying what needs to be said in hopes that, like the apostle Paul, "I might win some."[6]

Appendix

RELEVANT THOUGHTS
AND QUOTES

ALL THE FOLLOWING QUOTATIONS WERE FOUND IN THE
indispensable *America's God and Country: Encyclopedia of
Quotations*, compiled and annotated by William J. Federer.[1]

ON VIRTUE AND MORALITY

A general dissolution of principles and manners will
more surely overthrow the liberties of America than the
whole force of the common enemy. While the people are
virtuous they cannot be subdued; but when they lose
their virtue they will be ready to surrender their liberties
to the first external or internal invader.

—SAMUEL ADAMS,
in a letter to James Warren, February 12, 1779

Not until I went into the churches of America and heard
her pulpits flame with righteousness did I understand
the secret of her genius and power. America is great

because America is good, and if America ever ceases to be good, America will cease to be great.

—ALEXIS DE TOCQUEVILLE

Let the religious element in a man's nature be neglected, let him be influenced by no higher motives than low self-interest, and subjected to no stronger restraint than the limits of civil authority, and he becomes the creature of selfish passion or blind fanaticism.

—DANIEL WEBSTER,
in a speech, July 4, 1851

The only assurance of our nation's safety is to lay our foundation in morality and religion.

—ABRAHAM LINCOLN

History fails to record a single precedent in which nations subject to moral decay have not passed into political and economic decline. There has been either a spiritual awakening to overcome the moral lapse, or a progressive deterioration leading to ultimate national disaster.

—GENERAL DOUGLAS MACARTHUR

Modern man has not only thrown away Christian theology, he has thrown away the possibility of what our forefathers had as a basis for morality and law.

—FRANCIS SCHAEFFER,
in *Escape From Reason*, 1968

America was founded by people who believed that God was their rock of safety. I recognize we must be cautious in claiming that God is on our side, but I think it's all right to keep asking if we're on His side.

—RONALD REAGAN,
January 25, 1984

ON CHRISTIANITY AND RELIGION

The Christian religion is, above all Religions that ever prevailed or existed in ancient or modern times, the religion of Wisdom, Virtue, Equity, and Humanity...it is Goodness itself to Man.

—JOHN ADAMS,
an entry in his diary dated July 26, 1796

Christianity works while infidelity talks. She feeds the hungry, clothes the naked, visits and cheers the sick, and seeks the lost, while infidelity abuses her and babbles nonsense and profanity. "By their fruits ye shall know them."

—HENRY WARD BEECHER,
abolitionist editor and publisher

I believe that the next half century will determine if we will advance the cause of Christian civilization or revert to the horrors of brutal paganism. The thought of modern industry in the hands of Christian charity is a dream worth dreaming. The thought of industry in the hands of paganism is a nightmare beyond imagining. The choice between the two is upon us.

—THEODORE ROOSEVELT,
1909

We have been the recipients of the choicest bounties of Heaven. We have been preserved these many years in peace and prosperity. We have grown in numbers, wealth and power as no other nation has ever grown. But we have forgotten God....Intoxicated with unbroken success, we have become too self-sufficient to feel the

necessity of redeeming and preserving grace, too proud
to pray to the God that made us!

—ABRAHAM LINCOLN,
in his historic Proclamation
Appointing a National Fast Day,
March 30, 1863

The time has come to turn to God and reassert our trust
in Him for healing of America...our country is in need
of and ready for a spiritual renewal.

—RONALD REAGAN

ON THE BIBLE

The first and almost the only Book deserving of uni-
versal attention is the Bible.

—JOHN QUINCY ADAMS

That book, Sir, is the Rock upon which our republic rests.

—ANDREW JACKSON,
referring to the Bible,
June 8, 1845

You are wrong, Speed. Take all that you can of this book
[the Bible] upon reason, and the balance on faith, and
you will live and die a happier man.

—ABRAHAM LINCOLN
to a skeptical friend, Joshua Speed,
who commented upon seeing Lincoln reading the Bible

The more profoundly we study this wonderful Book,
and the more closely we observe its divine precepts, the
better citizens we will become and the higher will be our
destiny as a nation.

—WILLIAM MCKINLEY

I am sorry for the men who do not read the Bible every day. I wonder why they deprive themselves of the strength and of the pleasure.

—WOODROW WILSON

We cannot read the history of our rise and development as a nation, without reckoning with the place the Bible has occupied in shaping the advances of the Republic.... [W]here we have been the truest and most consistent in obeying its precepts, we have attained the greatest measure of contentment and prosperity.

—FRANKLIN D. ROOSEVELT,
in a 1935 radio broadcast

ON COURAGE AND CONVICTION

All that is necessary for evil to triumph is for good men to do nothing.

—EDMUND BURKE,
in a letter to William Smith,
January 9, 1795

Patriotism, honor, glory, and national prosperity, are terms to which the Christian and the mere politician attach different ideas, and estimate by different standards. He who admits the authority of the Bible will not readily acknowledge that whatever is "highly esteemed among men" must be right, nor that which is unpopular is, of course, wrong.

—WILLIAM JAY,
abolitionist and son of John Jay,
the first Chief Justice of the Supreme Court

The true Christian is the true citizen, lofty of purpose, resolute in endeavor, ready for a hero's deeds, but never looking down on his task because it is cast in the day of small things.

—THEODORE ROOSEVELT

SUGGESTED READING

Barna, George. *Revolution: Worn Out on Church*. Wheaton, IL: Tyndale House Publishers, Inc., 2005.

Barton, David. *Original Intent: The Courts, the Constitution, & Religion*. Aledo, TX: WallBuilder Press, 2000.

————. *The Bible, Voters, and the 2008 Election*. Aledo, TX: WallBuilder Press, 2008.

Blumenfeld, Samuel L. *NEA: Trojan Horse in American Education*. Boise, ID: The Paradigm Co., 1984.

Chambers, Alan. *God's Grace and the Homosexual Next Door*. Eugene, OR: Harvest House Publishers, 2006.

Colson, Charles. *God and Government*. Grand Rapid, MI: Zondervan, 2007.

DeMar, Gary. *Thinking Straight in a Crooked World*. Powder Springs, GA: American Vision, 2001.

————. *Whoever Controls the Schools Rules the World*. Powder Springs, GA: American Vision, 2007.

Federer, William J. *America's God and Country Encyclopedia of Quotations*. Coppell, TX: FAME Publishing, Inc., 1994.

————. *The Ten Commandments and Their Influence on American Law*. St. Louis, MO: Amerisearch, Inc., 2003.

Folger, Janet L. *The Criminalization of Christianity*. Sisters, OR: Multnomah Publishers, 2005.

Ham, Ken et al. *No Retreats, No Reserves, No Regrets: Why Christians Should Never Give Up, Never Hold Back, and Never Be Sorry When Proclaiming Their Faith*. St. Paul, MN: Stewart House Press, 2000.

Howse, Brannon. *Put Your Beliefs to the Test*. Collierville, TN: Worldview Weekend Publishing, 2006.

————. *Christian Worldview for Students*, vols. 1 and 2. Collierville, TN: Worldviews Weekend Publishing, 2006, 2008.

Kern, Steve. *No Other Gods: The Biblical Creation Worldview*. St. Louis, MO: Amerisearch, Inc., 2007.

Kirk, Marshall and Erastes Pill. "The Overhauling of Straight America." *Guide*, November 1987.

Kirk, Marshall and Hunter Madsen. *After the Ball: How America Can Conquer Its Fear and Hatred of Gays in the 90s*. New York: Plume Publisher, 1989.

Kupelian, David. *The Marketing of Evil*. Nashville, TN: Cumberland House Publishers, Inc., 2005.

Maglio, Domenick J. *Invasion Within*. Washington DC: Regnery Publishing, Inc., 2005.

McDowell, Josh and Bob Hostetler. *Right From Wrong*. Dallas, TX: Word Publishing, 1994.

Noebel, David. *Understanding the Times: The Story of the Biblical Christian, Marxist/Leninist and Secular Humanist Worldviews*. Manitou Springs, CO: Summit Press, 1991.

Parshall, Janet and Craig. *The Light in the City.* Nashville, TN: Thomas Nelson Publishers, 2000.

Pearcey, Nancy. *Total Truth.* Wheaton, IL: Crossway Books, 2004.

Quist, Allen. *FedEd: The New Federal Curriculum and How It's Enforced.* St. Paul, MN: Maple River Education Coalition, 2002.

Schmierer, Don and Lela Gilbert. *An Ounce of Prevention: Preventing the Homosexual Condition in Today's Youth.* Santa Ana, CA: Promise Publishing Co., 2002.

Sears, Alan and Craig Osten. *The Homosexual Agenda.* Nashville, TN: Broadman and Holman Publishers, 2003.

Sheldon, Louis P. *The Agenda: The Homosexual Plan to Change America.* Lake Mary, FL: FrontLine, 2005.

Sprigg, Peter. *Outrage: How Gay Activists and Liberal Judges Are Trashing Democracy to Redefine Marriage.* Washington DC: Regnery Publishing, Inc., 2004.

Staver, Mat D. *Same-Sex Marriage: Putting Every Household at Risk.* Nashville, TN: Broadman and Holman Publishers, 2004.

NOTES

CHAPTER 1
"GOOD LORD, WHAT HAVE I DONE?"

1. As quoted in T. DeWitt Talmadge, ed., *Frank Leslie's Sunday Magazine*, vol. 24 (New York: Frank Leslie's Publishing House, 1888), 234, viewed at Google Books.

CHAPTER 2
THE SPEECH THAT GOT IT STARTED

1. Rosie O'Donnell statement on ABC's *The View*, September 12, 2006.

CHAPTER 4
THE RAGING FIRESTORMS

1. John Corvino, "Corvino: Beyond Tolerance," 365gay.com, August 15, 2008, http://www.365gay.com/opinion/081508-corvino-tolerance/ (accessed February 2, 2011).

2. Brian Brus, "OKC Chamber: Kern Spooks Big Biz Relocation Consultant," *Journal Record*, April 16, 2008, abstract viewed at http://journalrecord.com/2008/04/16/okc-chamber-kern-spooks-big-biz-relocation-consultant/ (accessed February 2, 2011).

3. Ibid.

4. Ibid.

5. Editorial Staff, "Sally Kern Is Bad for Business," *Journal Record*, July 8, 2009.

6. Alec Foege, "Best Places to Launch," *Fortune Small Business*, October 2009, http://money.cnn.com/smallbusiness/best_places_launch/2009/snapshot/241.html (accessed January 26, 2011).

CHAPTER 5
THE TROOPS RALLY

1. Michael McNutt, "Hundreds Gather to Protest Kern's Comments," *The Oklahoman*, March 18, 2008, abstract viewed at http://newsok.com/article/3217675/1205868195 (accessed January 26, 2011).

2. Ibid.

3. Ibid.

4. "Freedom of Speech Rally for Sally," March 17, 2008.

5. Anita Bryant Ministries International, "Anita Bryant Biography," http://www.anitabmi.org/3.html (accessed February 10, 2011).

6. Yolanne Almanzar, "Florida Gay Adoption Is Ruled Unconstitutional," *New York Times*, November 25, 2008, http://www.nytimes.com/2008/11/26/us/26florida.html?_r=1 (accessed March 2, 2011).

7. Ibid.

8. Anita Bryant, *The Anita Bryant Story* (n.p.: Revell, 1977), 15.

CHAPTER 6
CAUTION! DANGER AHEAD!

1. National Transportation Safety Board, Safety Recommendation, September 8, 2004, http://www.ntsb.gov/recs/letters/2004/H04_31.pdf (accessed February 2, 2011).

2. Mike Lambeth, "Tragedy on I-40," *Game & Fish*, www.gameandfishmag.com/fishing/bass-fishing/gf_aa016503a/ (accessed February 2, 2011).

3. Marshall K. Kirk and Erastes Pill, "The Overhauling of Straight America," *Guide Magazine*, November 1987.

4. Stanley Kurtz, "Dissolving Marriage: If Everything Is Marriage, Then Nothing Is," *National Review Online*, February 3, 2006 http://old .nationalreview.com/kurtz/kurtz200602030805.asp (accessed January 18, 2011).

5. Kirk and Pill, "The Overhauling of Straight America."

6. Ibid.

7. Ibid.

8. Ibid.

9. Ibid.

10. Ibid.

11. Marshall Kirk and Hunter Madsen, *After the Ball: How America Will Conquer Its Fear and Hatred of Gays in the '90s* (New York: Plume, 1990), xxviii.

12. Ibid., 184.

13. GLSEN.org, "Back-to-School Guide for Creating LGBT Inclusive Environments," August 26, 2010, http://www.glsen.org/cgi-bin/iowa/all/ library/record/2614.html (accessed February 14, 2011).

14. Brian J. Burt, "'Gay' Leader Kevin Jennings Says Dream Is to 'Promote Homosexuality' in Schools," *Lambda Report*, January/February 1998, as reported on Americans for Truth, http://americans fortruth.com/news/%E2%80%98gay%E2%80%99-leader-kevin-jennings -says-dream-is-to-%E2%80%98promote-homosexuality%E2%80%99-in -schools.html (accessed February 14, 2011).

15. Scott Whiteman, "The 'Fistgate' Tapes, Part 1," MassResistance .com, June 15, 2009, http://www.massresistance.org/docs/issues/fistgate/ tape01.html (accessed February 21, 2011).

16. Ibid.

17. William J. Letts IV and James T. Sears, *Queering Elementary Education: Advancing the Dialogue About Sexualities and Schooling* (Lanham, MD: Rowman & Littlefield Publishers, 1999), 260.

18. Kevin Jennings, *Mama's Boy, Preacher's Son: A Memoir* (Boston, MA: Beacon Press, 2007).

19. David Brown, "HIV Rate Up 12 Percent Among Young Gay Men," *Washington Post*, June 27, 2008, http://www.washingtonpost.com/wp-dyn/content/article/2008/06/26/AR2008062603521.html (accessed February 14, 2011).

20. H. Weinstock, S. Berman, and W. Cates, "Sexually Transmitted Diseases Among American Youth: Incidence and Prevalence Estimates, 2000," *Perspectives on Sexual and Reproductive Health* 36, no. 1 (2004): 6–10, reported in Centers for Disease Control and Prevention, "Sexual Risk Behaviors," http://www.cdc.gov/HealthyYouth/sexualbehaviors/index.htm (accessed February 14, 2011).

21. Lisa Miller, "Our Mutual Joy," *Newsweek*, December 6, 2008, http://www.newsweek.com/2008/12/05/our-mutual-joy.html (accessed February 21, 2011).

22. TripAtlas.com, "Folsom Street Fair," http://tripatlas.com/Folsom_Street_Fair (accessed February 21, 2011).

23. Ibid.

24. Louis P. Sheldon, *The Agenda: The Homosexual Plan to Change America* (Lake Mary, FL: FrontLine, 2005), 47.

25. *The Report*, "There Goes Freedom of Religion: Canadian Courts and Government Continue to Drive Faith Out of the Public Square, Right by Right," June 10, 2002, http://www.highbeam.com/doc/1G1-90631344.html (accessed February 21, 2011). Also, Ed Vilagliamo, "Gay Activists War Against Christianity," *American Family Association Journal*, February 2006, http://www.afajournal.org/2006/february/206GayWar.asp (accessed January 18, 2011).

26. Paula Ettelbrick, "Since When Is Marriage a Path to Liberation?" *OUT/LOOK*, Fall 1989, in Andrew Sullivan, *Same-Sex Marriage: Pro and Con* (New York: Random House, 2004).

27. Steve Warren, "Warning to the Homophobes," *The Advocate*, September 1, 1987, as quoted in Ed Vitagliano, "Gay Activists' War Against Christianity," *American Family Association Journal*, February

2006, http://www.afajournal.org/2006/february/206GayWar.asp (accessed February 25, 2011).

28. National Association for Research and Therapy of Homosexuality, "Is There a 'Gay Gene'?" www.narth.com/docs/istheregene.html (accessed February 15, 2011); WebMD, "Is There a 'Gay Gene'?" January 28, 2005, http://www.webmd.com/sex-relationships/news/20050128/is-there-gay-gene (accessed February 15, 2011).

29. Dale O'Leary, "Childhood Experiences of Homosexual Men," Fathers for Life, http://fathersforlife.org/dale/childhood_of_homosexual_men_2.htm (accessed February 15, 2011).

30. Kathleen A. Kendall-Tackett, *Handbook of Women, Stress, and Trauma* (New York: Brunner-Routledge, 2004), 256.

31. Robert H. Knight, "Born or Bred? Science Does Not Support the Claim That Homosexuality Is Genetic," Concerned Women for America, June 2009, http://www.cwfa.org/articledisplay.asp?id=5458 (accessed February 3, 2011).

32. Abraham Lincoln, "Lyceum Address," January 27, 1838, Founding.com (a project of the Claremont Institute), http://www.founding.com/publications/pageID.2626/default.asp (accessed January 18, 2011).

CHAPTER 7
MORALITY, TRUTH, AND TOLERANCE

1. Library of Congress, "Religion and the Founding of the American Republic," http://www.loc.gov/exhibits/religion/rel04.html (accessed February 21, 2011), with document at http://www.loc.gov/exhibits/religion/f0404s.jpg (viewed February 21, 2011).

2. "Oklahoma Citizens' Proclamation for Morality," July 2, 2009, http://www.repsallykern.com/html/news_details.php?id=36 (accessed February 11, 2011).

3. Charles Francis Adams, ed., *The Works of John Adams—Second President of the United States*, vol. 9 (Boston: Little, Brown, & Co., 1854), 401.

4. Ibid., 228–229.

5. Ibid., 229.

6. Frederick Nymeyer, *Progressive Calvinism*, vol. 4 (1958), 31. While some question the attribution of this statement to Madison, conservative Christian historians say it is in line with other statements Madison made.

7. William S. Pfaff, ed., *Maxims & Morals of Benjamin Franklin* (New Orleans: Searcy and Pfaff, Ltd., 1927).

8. Thomas Jefferson, "A Summary View of the Rights of British America," in Julian P. Boyd et al., *The Papers of Thomas Jefferson* (Princeton, NJ: Princeton University Press, 1950). See also "Quotations on the Jefferson Memorial," http://www.monticello.org/site/jefferson/quotations-jefferson-memorial (accessed February 21, 2011).

9. Thomas Jefferson, *Notes on the State of Virginia*, query 18, (1781), 289, viewed at http://etext.virginia.edu/etcbin/toccer-new2?id=JefVirg.sgm&images=images/modeng&data=/texts/english/modeng/parsed&tag=public&part=all (accessed February 21, 2011). See also "Quotations on the Jefferson Memorial," http://www.monticello.org/site/jefferson/quotations-jefferson-memorial (accessed February 21, 2011).

10. Joseph Story, *Commentaries on the Constitution*, vol. 3, sec. 1868 and 1869 (New York: Da Capo Press, 1970), 726–727; originally published 1833.

11. Christopher Collier, *Roger Sherman's Connecticut* (Middletown, CT: Wesleyan University Press, 1979), 129.

12. Steve C. Dawson, *God's Providence in America's History*, vol. 1 (Rancho Cordova, CA: Steve C. Dawson, 1988), 5. While some question the attribution of this statement to Henry, conservative Christian historians say it is in line with other statements Henry made.

13. Noah Webster, *History of the United States* (New Haven, CT: Durrie and Peck, 1832), 336.

14. Noah Webster, ed., *The Holy Bible, Containing the Old and New Testaments, in the Common Version. With Amendments of the Language* (New Haven, CT: Durrie and Peck, 1833), 160. Reprinted by Baker Book House, Grand Rapids, MI (1987).

15. "Blessed is the nation whose God is the LORD" (Ps. 33:12, KJV).

16. David Barton, as quoted in Arkansas Patriot, "A Courageous State Leader," September 2009, http://arkansaspatriot.us/2009/09/28/a-courageous-state-leader/ (accessed February 3, 2011).

17. Josh McDowell and Bob Hostetler, *Right From Wrong* (Dallas, TX: Word Publishing, 1994), 17.

18. Barna Group, "How America's Faith Has Changed Since 9-11," http://www.barna.org/barna-update/article/5-barna-update/63-how-americas-faith-has-changed-since-9-11 (accessed February 24, 2011).

19. Barna Group, "Americans Are Most Likely to Base Truth on Feelings" http://www.barna.org/barna-update/article/5-barna-update/67-americans-are-most-likely-to-base-truth-on-feelings (accessed January 18, 2011).

20. Barna Group, "Barna Survey Examines Changes in Worldview Among Christians Over the Past 13 Years."

21. As reported in John O'Sullivan, "Retraction Required," National Review Online, September 25, 2001, http://old.nationalreview.com/jos/josprint092501.html (accessed January 18, 2011).

22. Thomas Hargrove, "Third of Americans Suspect 9/11 Government Conspiracy," Scripps Howard News Service, August 1, 2006, http://www.scrippsnews.com/911poll (accessed January 18, 2011).

23. As related in Philip Yancey, *Soul Survivor* (Colorado Springs, CO: WaterBrook Press, 2001).

24. John Newton, *The Works of John Newton... to which are prefixed memoirs of his life* (Charleston, SC: Nabu Press, 2010).

25. Massachusetts Historical Society, Adams Family Papers, Diaries of John Adams, http://www.masshist.org/digitaladams/aea/cfm/doc.cfm?id=D16 (accessed February 25, 2011).

26. Human Rights Panels of Alberta, "Darren E. Lund (complainant) and Stephen Boissoin and the Concerned Christian Coalition Inc. (respondent) and Canadian Civil Liberties Association and Attorney General of Alberta (interveners): Decision," November 30, 2007, http://www.albertahumanrights.ab.ca/LundDarren113007Pa.pdf (accessed February 25, 2011).

27. Boissoin v. Lund, 2009 ABQB 592, http://www.albertacourts
.ab.ca/jdb%5C2003-%5Cqb%5Cciv il%5C2009%5C2009abqb0592.pdf
(accessed January 26, 2011).

28. Bob Unruh. "Obama Ripped for Plan to Bring Back 'Inquisi-
tions,'" WorldNetDaily.com, December 13, 2009, http://www.wnd
.com/?pageId=118710 (accessed January 18, 2011).

29. G. K. Chesterton, *The Collected Works of G. K. Chesterton*, vol.
31 (San Francisco: Ignatius Press, 1989), 76.

30. Brian Erwin. "Redefining Hate," *Urban Tulsa Weekly*, March 19,
2008, http://www.urbantulsa.com/gyrobase/Content?oid=oid%3A20327
(accessed February 25, 2011).

31. Jesse McKinley, "Theater Director Resigns Amid Gay-Rights
Ire," *New York Times*, November 12, 2008, http://www.nytimes.com/
2008/11/13/theater/13thea.html (accessed January 18, 2011).

32. Rachel Abramowitz, "Film Fest Director Resigns," *Los Angeles
Times*, November 26, 2008, http://articles.latimes.com/2008/nov/26/
entertainment/et-raddonresigns26 (accessed January 18, 2011).

33. Alison Stateman, "What Happens If You're on Gay Rights' 'Enemies List,'" *Time*, November 15, 2008, http://www.time.com/time/nation/
article/0,8599,1859323,00.html (accessed January 18, 2011).

34. Warren Richey, "Nativity Scene Is Too Religious for New York
City Schools," *Christian Science Monitor*, February 22, 2007, http://www
.csmonitor.com/2007/0222/p04s01-ussc.html (accessed January 26, 2011).

35. Matthew Spolar, "Sign for Jesus Plan Revived," *Concord Monitor*,
October 7, 2010, http://www.concordmonitor.com/article/219401/sign
-for-jesus-plan-revived (accessed March 29, 2011).

36. Bob Unruh, "Firing for Being 'Too Religious' Challenged,"
WorldNetDaily.com, October 28, 2010, http://www.wnd
.com/?pageId=221009 (accessed March 29, 2011).

37. Perry Bacon Jr., "After 10-Year Dispute, Expansion of Hate
Crimes Law to Gays Signed," *Washington Post*, October 29, 2009,
http://www.washingtonpost.com/wp-dyn/content/article/2009/10/28/
AR2009102804909.html (accessed January 26, 2011).

38. News9.com, "ACLU Investigates Rep. Sally Kern," July 11, 2009, http://www.news9.com/Global/story.asp?S=10711924 (accessed February 15, 2011).

CHAPTER 8
RECLAIMING CHRISTIAN CONSERVATISM

1. Time.com, "The Crist Switch: Top 10 Political Defections—Ronald Reagan, 1962," http://www.time.com/time/specials/packages/article/0,28804,1894529_1894528_1894518,00.html (accessed February 15, 2011).

2. William W. Campbell, *The Life and Writings of De Witt Clinton* (New York: Baker and Scribner, 1849), 305.

3. David Barton, *The Practical Benefits of Christianity* (Aledo, TX: WallBuilders, 2001), 3.

4. Lester Jesse Cappon, *The Adams-Jefferson Letters* (Williamsburg, VA: Institute of Early American History and Culture, 1988), 340.

5. American Historical Association, *The American Historical Review*, vol. 11 (1906), 618.

6. James Madison, "Federalist No. 10—The Same Subject Continued: The Union as a Safeguard Against Domestic Faction and Insurrection," *The Federalist Papers*, http://thomas.loc.gov/home/histdox/fed_10.html (accessed February 25, 2011).

7. Noah Webster, *History of the United States* (New Haven, CT: Durie and Peck, 1832), 336–337; italics in original.

8. Noah Webster, *American Dictionary of the English Language*, 1828 facsimile edition (Chesapeake, VA: Foundation for American Christian Education, 1967), s.v. "politics."

9. Nymeyer, *Progressive Calvinism*, vol. 4 (1958), 31. While some question the attribution of this statement to Madison, conservative Christian historians say it is in line with other statements Madison made.

10. Sir William Blackstone, *Commentaries on the Laws of England, in four books*, vol. 1 (New York: n.p., 1832), 27.

11. Webster, *American Dictionary of the English Language*, 1828 facsimile edition.

12. Kurtz, "The End of Marriage in Scandinavia."

13. National Center for Fathering, "The Consequences of Fatherlessness," http://www.fathers.com/content/index.php?option=com_content&task=view&id=391 (accessed February 1, 2011).

14. John Adams and Charles Francis Adams, *The Works of John Adams, Second President of the United States*, vol. 9 (Boston, MA: Little, Brown and Company, 1854), 229.

15. John Locke, *Second Treatise of Government*, http://www.gutenberg.org/cache/epub/7370/pg7370.txt (accessed February 25, 2011).

16. Council on Foreign Relations, "Trinational Call for a North American Economic and Security Community by 2010," March 14, 2005, http://www.cfr.org/world/trinational-call-north-american-economic-security-community-2010/p7914 (accessed February 3, 2011).

17. Ronald Reagan, speaking at the Ecumenical Prayer Breakfast, Reunion Arena, Dallas, TX, August 23, 1984, http://www.americanrhetoric.com/speeches/ronaldreaganecumenicalprayer.htm (accessed February 25, 2011).

CHAPTER 9
FROM TYRANNY TO TYRANNY

1. McFarlane v. Relate Avon Ltd. [2010] EWCA Civ B1 (29 April 2010), http://www.bailii.org/ew/cases/EWCA/Civ/2010/B1.html (accessed February 25, 2011).

2. Sue Johnstone, "Reverend Masih v. AWAZ FM Limited (26 Aug 2009, ET/S/116403/08," Equal Opportunities Review, January 4, 2010, http://www.eortrial.co.uk/default.aspx?id=1127284 (accessed January 26, 2011).

3. Ladele v. London Borough of Islington [2009] EWCA Civ 1357 (15 December 2009), http://www.bailii.org/ew/cases/EWCA/Civ/2009/1357.html (accessed February 16, 2011).

4. Eweida v British Airways Plc [2010] EWCA Civ 80 (12 February 2010), http://www.bailii.org/ew/cases/EWCA/Civ/2010/80.html (accessed February 16, 2011).

5. Luke Salkeld, "Christian Nurse 'Ordered to Remove Crucifix...at Hospital Where Muslims Were Allowed to Wear Headscarves," *Daily Mail*, March 30, 2010, http://www.dailymail.co.uk/news/article-1261953/ Christian-nurse-Shirley-Chaplin-crucifix-row-Royal-Devon-Exeter -Hospital.html (accessed January 26, 2011).

6. Ruth Arlow and Will Adam, eds., "Noah v Desrosiers trading as Wedge," *Ecclesiastical Law Journal* 11 (2009): 233–234; abstract viewed at http://journals.cambridge.org/action/displayAbstract?fromPage=online &aid=5489848 (accessed February 25, 2011).

7. Sue Johnstone, "Almost £50,000 Awarded for Sexual Orientation Discrimination," Equal Opportunity Review, January 12, 2008, http:// www.rubensteinpublishing.com/default.aspx?id=1105802 (accessed February 25, 2011); BBC News, "Bishop Denies Gay Discrimination," April 4, 2007, http://news.bbc.co.uk/2/hi/uk_news/wales/6527347.stm (accessed March 4, 2011).

8. Glasgow City v. McNab, Appeal No. UKEATS/0037/06/MT, January 17, 2007, http://www.employmentappeals.gov.uk/Public/Upload/ UKEATS_0037_06_RN..doc (accessed February 16, 2011).

9. Catholic News Agency, "Ruling Forces Last Catholic Adoption Agency in England and Wales to Cease Adoptions," http://www .catholicnewsagency.com/news/ruling-forces-last-catholic-adoption -agency-in-england-and-wales-to-cease-adoptions (accessed February 25, 2011).

10. BBC News, "Christian Foster Couple Lose 'Homosexuality Views' Case," February 28, 2011, http://www.bbc.co.uk/news/uk -england-derbyshire-12598896 (accessed February 28, 2011). Also, Johns and Anor, R (on the application of) v. Derby City Council and Anor [2011] EWHC 375 (Admin) (28 February 2011), http://www.bailii.org/ew/ cases/EWHC/Admin/2011/375.html (accessed March 1, 2011).

11. Monica Furlong, *The C of E: The State It's In* (London: SPCK Publishing, Open Market Ed edition, 2006), 1.

12. Ibid., 210.

13. Jacinta Ashworth and Ian Farthing, "Churchgoing in the UK," Tearfund, April 2007, http://www.tearfund.org/webdocs/Website/News/Final%20churchgoing%20report.pdf (accessed January 26, 2011).

14. P. R. Hills, L. J. Francis, and P. Jennings, "Religious Behaviour, Personality and Dimensions of Self-Esteem Among 13- to 15-Year-Old Adolescents," *Journal of Research on Christian Education* 15, issue 1 (2006): 61–76.

15. Telegraph.co.uk, "Pope Benedict XVI Warns Against 'Aggressive Secularism' in Britain," September 16, 2010, http://www.telegraph.co.uk/news/newstopics/religion/the-pope/8006272/Pope-Benedict-XVI-warns-against-aggressive-secularism-in-Britain.html (accessed January 26, 2011).

16. Gallup.com, "Few Americans Oppose National Day of Prayer," May 5, 2010, http://www.gallup.com/poll/127721/Few-Americans-Oppose-National-Day-Prayer.aspx (accessed March 2, 2011).

17. Pew Forum on Religion and Public Life, "US Religious Landscape Survey," June 23, 2008, http://pewforum.org/US-Religious-Landscape-Survey-Resources.aspx (accessed January 26, 2011).

18. Frank Newport, "One-Third of Americans Believe the Bible Is Literally True."

19. Barna Group, "Most Twentysomethings Put Christianity on the Shelf Following Spiritually Active Teen Years," September 11, 2006, http://www.barna.org/barna-update/article/16-teensnext-gen/147-most-twentysomethings-put-christianity-on-the-shelf-following-spiritually-active-teen-years?q=twentysomethings+church (accessed January 26, 2011).

20. William Wetmore Story, ed., *Life and Letters of Joseph Story: Associate Justice of the Supreme Court and Dane Professor of Law at Harvard University* (Boston: Charles C. Little and James Brown, 1851), 546.

21. Francis A. Schaeffer, *A Christian Manifesto* (Wheaton, IL: Crossway Books, 2005).

22. Associated Press, "Oklahoma Sharia Law Blocked by Federal Judge," November 8, 2010, http://www.huffingtonpost.com/2010/11/08/oklahoma-sharia-law-struck-down-_n_780632.html (accessed February 25, 2011).

23. The Center for Security Policy, *Shariah: The Threat to America*, October 2010, http://www.centerforsecuritypolicy.org/upload/wysiwyg/article%20pdfs/Shariah%20-%20The%20Threat%20to%20America%20(Team%20B%20Report)%20Web%2009292010.pdf (accessed January 26, 2011); Maxim Lott, "Advocates of Anti-Shariah Measures Alarmed by Judge's Ruling," FoxNews.com, August 5, 2010, http://www.foxnews.com/us/2010/08/05/advocates-anti-shariah-measures-alarmed-judges-ruling/ (accessed March 2, 2011).

24. Parshall, "ENDA—Beginning of the End for Christian Dissent?"

25. Statement of Thomas E. Perez, Assistant Attorney General, Department of Justice at hearing entitled "Employment Non-Discrimination Act: Ensuring Opportunity for All Americans," November 5, 2009, http://help.senate.gov/imo/media/doc/Perez.pdf (accessed January 26, 2011).

26. National Hispanic Media Coalition, letter to Federal Communications Commission, May 7, 2010, http://fjallfoss.fcc.gov/ecfs/document/view?id=7020450549 (accessed January 26, 2011).

27. Letisia Marquez, "Preliminary Report Finds Extensive Use of Hate Speech on Conservative Talk Radio," UCLA Newsroom, January 28, 2009, http://newsroom.ucla.edu/portal/ucla/ucla-study-finds-extensive-use-79402.aspx (accessed February 25, 2011).

28. WorldNetDaily.com, "Homeland Security on Guard for 'Right-Wing Extremists,'" Office of Intelligence and Analysis, *Rightwing Extremism: Current Economic and Political Climate Fueling Resurgence in Radicalization and Recruitment.*

29. David Limbaugh, *Persecution: How Liberals Are Waging War Against Christianity* (Washington DC: Regnery Publishing, 2004), 27–33. Examples include: Cheryl Caswell, "Many Upset About Exclusion of Prayer at One Commencement," *Charleston Daily Mail*, December 17, 2010, http://www.dailymail.com/News/statenews/201012160752 (accessed

February 28, 2011); FoxNews.com, "Valedictorian Sues to Stop High School Prayer," March 11, 2010, http://www.foxnews.com/us/2010/03/11/ valedictorian-sues-stop-high-school-graduation-prayer/ (accessed February 28, 2011); Lee v. Weisman, 505 U.S. 577 (1992), viewed at Cornell University Law School, http://www.law.cornell.edu/supct/html/90-1014 .ZS.html (accessed February 28, 2011).

30. Limbaugh, *Persecution: How Liberals Are Waging War Against Christianity*, 22–27. Examples include: Santa Fe Independent School District v. Doe, No. 99-62 (2000), viewed at FindLaw.com, http://caselaw .lp.findlaw.com/cgi-bin/getcase.pl?court=US&navby=case&vol=000&i nvol=99-62 (accessed February 28, 2011).

31. Limbaugh, *Persecution: How Liberals Are Waging War Against Christianity*, 50–53. Examples include: Lindsay Toler, "High Court Won't Hear Kent Schools Bible-Club Case," *Seattle Times*, June 30, 2009, http://seattletimes.nwsource.com/html/localnews/2009400011_ bibleclub30mo.html (accessed February 28, 2011); Joshua Rhett Miller, "Christian Group Allowed to Return to Ohio Campus," FoxNews.com, March 3, 2009, http://www.foxnews.com/story/0,2933,504115,00.html (accessed February 28, 2011); My-Thuan Tran, "School Must Allow Bible Club," *Los Angeles Times*, September 4, 2008, http://articles.latimes .com/2008/sep/04/local/me-bible4 (accessed February 28, 2011).

32. Thomas Jefferson, *Writings*, Merrill D. Patterson, ed. (New York: Literary Classics of the United States, Inc., 1984), 1426.

33. Oliver Wendell Holmes Jr., *The Common Law* (Boston: Little, Brown, and Company, 1881), 1.

34. Alexander Hamilton, "Federalist No. 78," *The Federalist Papers*, Library of Congress, http://thomas.loc.gov/home/histdox/fed_78.html (accessed February 28, 2011).

35. Dan Fletcher, "A Brief History of the Fairness Doctrine," *Time*, February 20, 2009, http://www.time.com/time/nation/ article/0,8599,1880786,00.html (accessed February 16, 2011).

36. Josiah Ryan, "Speaker Pelosi Backs Senate Amendment to Regulate Talk Radio," CNSNews.com, March 5, 2009, http://www.cnsnews .com/news/article/44588 (accessed February 16, 2011).

37. Declaration of Independence, National Archives and Records Administration, http://www.archives.gov/exhibits/charters/declaration _transcript.html (accessed February 15, 2011).

CHAPTER 10
THE WAR AT SCHOOL

1. Nancy R. Pearcey, *Total Truth* (Wheaton, IL: Crossway Books, 2004).

2. Gary DeMar, *Whoever Controls the Schools Rules the World* (Powder Springs, GA: American Vision, 2007), 1.

3. William J. Federer, *America's God and Country: Encyclopedia of Quotations* (St. Louis, MO: Amerisearch, Inc, 2000), 391.

4. John Dewey, *The School and Society: Being Three Lectures* (Chicago: University of Chicago Press, 1899), 25.

5. John Dewey, *My Pedagogic Creed* (New York: E. L. Kellogg & Co., 1897), 10.

6. Ibid., 7, 9.

7. Benjamin Bloom, *All Our Children Learning* (n.p.: McGraw-Hill, 1981), 180.

8. B. F. Skinner, *Beyond Freedom and Dignity* (New York: Hachette Publishing Co., 1971), 207.

9. School-to-Work Opportunities Act of 1994, Public Law 103-239, May 4, 1994, http://www.fessler.com/SBE/act.htm (accessed March 2, 2011).

10. National Education Association, "2009-2010 NEA Resolutions," http://tinyurl.com/5v3bgjj (accessed February 2, 2011).

11. Alliance for Excellent Education, "How Does the United States Stack Up?", March 2008, http://www.all4ed.org/files/IntlComp_ FactSheet.pdf (accessed February 1, 2011).

12. Amanda K. Miller and Kathryn Chandler, "Violence in U.S. Public Schools," National Center for Education Statistics, October 2003, rev. August 2005, http://nces.ed.gov/pubs2004/2004314.pdf (accessed February 1, 2011).

13. Brannon Howse, "Dead Men Roam School Hallways," in Ken Ham et al., *No Retreats, No Reserves, No Regrets* (St. Paul, MN: Stewart House Press, 2000), 121.

14. From a keynote address to the Association for Childhood Education International, Denver, Colorado, April 1972, quoted by John Steinbacher and Dr. Dennis Cuddy, as referenced in Howse, "Dead Men Roam School Hallways," 121.

15. David Barton, "Pro-Family Legislators Conference," October 2007.

16. Joseph Alden, "The Young Citizen's Manual," in *Alden's Citizen's Manual: A Text-Book on Government, for Common Schools* (New York and Chicago: Sheldon & Company, 1869), 7, 9.

17. Paul Vitz, *Censorship: Evidence of Bias in Our Children's Textbooks* (Ann Arbor, MI: Servant Books, 1986), 1.

18. Transcript of speech given by Shirley McCune at Governor's Conference on Education, Wichita, Kansas, November 2, 1989, http://www.crossroad.to/Quotes/Education/ShirleyMcCune.htm (accessed March 1, 2011). Also quoted in Michael J. Chapman, "Worldview War in the Classroom," in Ham et al., *No Retreats, No Reserves, No Regrets*, 133.

19. Charles F. Potter, *Humanism: A New Religion* (New York: Simon & Schuster, 1930), 128.

20. Carole Gupton et al., "University of Minnesota Teacher Education Redesign Initiative, Race, Culture, Class, and Gender Task Group Report," July 16, 2009, http://thefire.org/article/11314.html (accessed February 16, 2011); Diane Macedo, "University of Minnesota Under Fire for Task Force's Discrimination-Based Teacher Education Plan," FoxNews.com, December 10, 2009, http://www.foxnews.com/us/2009/12/10/university-minnesota-task-forces-discrimination-based-teacher-education-plan/ (accessed February 16, 2011).

21. Ibid.

22. Phyllis Schlafly, "'Social Justice': Code Word for Anti-Americanism," Eagle Forum, January 2009, http://www.eagleforum.org/psr/2009/jan09/psrjan09.html (accessed January 31, 2011).

23. Ibid.

24. Dinitia Smith, "No Regrets for a Love of Explosives; In a Memoir of Sorts, a War Protester Talks of Life With the Weathermen," *New York Times*, September 11, 2001, http://query.nytimes.com/gst/fullpage.html?res=9F02E1DE1438F932A2575AC0A9679C8B63 (accessed February 16, 2011).

25. Ibid.

26. 1 Annals of Congress 729–731 (August 15, 1789), referenced in Cornell University Law School, "First Amendment: Religion and Expression," CRS Annotated Constitution, http://www.law.cornell.edu/anncon/html/amdt1afrag1_user.html#fnb2ref (accessed March 1, 2011).

27. National Archives, "Bill of Rights," http://www.archives.gov/exhibits/charters/bill_of_rights_transcript.html (accessed March 1, 2011).

28. Fisher Ames, *Palladium*, September 20, 1789, as quoted in William J. Federer, *America's God and Country: Encyclopedia of Quotations* (Coppell, TX: FAME Publishing, Inc., 1994), 26.

29. Ian Urbina, "Teacher With Bible Divides Ohio Town," *New York Times*, January 19, 2010, http://www.nytimes.com/2010/01/20/education/20teacher.html (accessed February 17, 2011).

30. John Quincy Adams, *Letters of John Quincy Adams to His Son on the Bible and Its Teaching* (Auburn, NY: Derby, Miller, & Co., 1848), 17–18.

31. William Wirt, *Sketches of the Life and Character of Patrick Henry* (Philadelphia: James Webster, 1817), 402.

32. Chau Lam, "Lindenhurst School District Settles Bible Club Lawsuit," Newsday.com, October 4, 2009, http://www.newsday.com/long-island/suffolk/lindenhurst-school-district-settles-bible-club-lawsuit-1.1499838 (accessed February 17, 2011).

33. Cooperation Agreement Between the United Nations Educational, Scientific and Cultural Organization and Microsoft Corporation, November 17, 2004, as viewed at http://www.eagleforum.org/links/UNESCO-MS.pdf (accessed February 17, 2011).

34. Crumley, "U.S. Conservatives Attack UNESCO's Sex-Ed Guidelines," United Nations Educational, Scientific and Cultural Organization, *International Technical Guidance on Sexuality Education.*

35. Ibid.

CONCLUSION
FALL BACK? NOT HARDLY

1. Martin, "And Now, a Rant: Christians Can't Be Happy Unless They're Making Gays Unhappy," *Atheist Experience* (blog), December 20, 2008, http://atheistexperience.blogspot.com/2008/12/and-now-rant -christians-cant-be-happy.html (accessed March 1, 2011).

2. Stephanie Pappas, "Church-Goers Tend to be Happier People," MSNBC.com, December 7, 2010, http://today.msnbc.msn.com/ id/40557983/ns/today-today_health (accessed February 18, 2011).

3. First Stone Ministries, http://www.firststone.org/ (accessed February 18, 2011).

4. Focus Action/LFF article, "The Cabinet," November 11, 2008.

5. George Washington, "Inaugural Address of 1789," National Archives and Records Administration, April 30, 1789, http://www .archives.gov/exhibits/american_originals/inaugtxt.html (accessed February 17, 2011).

6. "For although I am free from all people, I have made myself a slave to all, in order to win more people. To the Jews I became like a Jew, to win Jews; to those under the law, like one under the law— though I myself am not under the law—to win those under the law. To those who are outside the law, like one outside the law—not being outside God's law, but under the law of Christ—to win those outside the law. To the weak I became weak, in order to win the weak. I have become all things to all people, so that I may by all means save some" (1 Cor. 9:19–22).

Appendix
Relevant Thoughts and Quotes

1. William J. Federer, *America's God and Country: Encyclopedia of Quotations* (Coppell, TX: FAME Publishing, Inc., 1994).

INDEX

FREE NEWSLETTERS
TO HELP EMPOWER YOUR LIFE

Why subscribe today?

❏ **DELIVERED DIRECTLY TO YOU.** All you have to do is open your inbox and read.

❏ **EXCLUSIVE CONTENT.** We cover the news overlooked by the mainstream press.

❏ **STAY CURRENT.** Find the latest court rulings, revivals, and cultural trends.

❏ **UPDATE OTHERS.** Easy to forward to friends and family with the click of your mouse.

CHOOSE THE E-NEWSLETTER THAT INTERESTS YOU MOST:

- Christian news
- Daily devotionals
- Spiritual empowerment
- And much, much more

SIGN UP AT: **http://freenewsletters.charismamag.com**

8178